ARMY
AVIATION

ARMY AVIATION

Hans Halberstadt

Presidio Press ★ Novato, California

THE PRESIDIO POWER SERIES
LANDPOWER #3006

This book is dedicated to two Army aviators of the old school, my father, M. Halberstadt, 2d Lt., U.S. Army Air Corps, and my father-in-law, John Hope, 2d Lt., U.S. Army Air Corps, with thanks to both, for everything.

Published by Presidio Press
31 Pamaron Way, Novato CA 94949

Library of Congress Cataloging-in-Publication Data

Halberstadt, Hans.
    Army aviation / Hans Halberstadt.
       p. cm.—(The Presidio power series. Landpower ; #3006)
    ISBN 0-89141-251-4
    1. United States. Army—Aviation. 2. Military helicopters-
-United States. 3. Airmobile operations. 4. Close air support.
    I. Title. II. Series.
    UG633.H34   1989
    358.4'00973—dc20   89-16291
                                    CIP

Quality printing and binding by Ringier America / New Berlin
16555 West Rogers Drive, New Berlin WI 93151

Contents

Preface

I joined the Army when I was eighteen, and it was my privilege and (looking back on it) pleasure to be part of that institution at a critical point in its evolution. That was way back in 1962, and it was the beginning of the current era of aviation, Army style. I got to watch it change, from the inside, and participate to the extent that junior enlisted soldiers ever do: by greasing and guarding things, staying out of the way, doing as I was told, and watching the play unfold.

Back in early 1962, even in the Army, the fight in Viet Nam was barely a rumor; we knew something was happening across the Pacific, but we weren't sure what, and we weren't sure why. Our instructors in basic training and then at the Army Aviation Center mentioned the place from time to time, as an incentive to pay attention. But nobody really knew where the place was or just what kind of fighting Americans were doing there. It was obvious, however, that that was where the action was, and that's what I put down for my first choice when we filled out our "dream sheets" after completing helicopter maintenance school. And that's where I went, back in October of 1962, when you had to have a passport to go. We were the first replacements for the H-21 crews who had already fought there for nearly a year.

The place, back then, was deliciously exotic: new sights and smells and experiences, all seasoned with the ever present danger of Viet Cong (VC) mischief. There were fourteen thousand Americans when I arrived, not a lot more when I left. It was not really our show. This war, we discovered, had been going on for a long time before we arrived, and we were under no illusions about it concluding in the near future.

My assignment was to the 8th Transportation Helicopter Company several hundred miles north of Saigon in a small coastal city called Qui Nhon. Later it would become a big, bustling hub for American activity in the region, but at the time it was a sleepy little place, and there were few of us to disturb its peace. We climbed down from the USAF C-123 transport that brought us and were face to face with a dozen H-21s in fresh camouflage paint, a barbed wire compound, and a few low buildings of local design. That was the 8th Trans, and that was just about all the American war effort for a hundred miles in any direction.

At the first possible moment, several of us presented ourselves at the supply room and drew our flight gear: helmet, flak jacket, knife, survival radio—and a morphine Syrette. All this plus the usual field equipment the Army loans its members: steel pot, web gear, poncho, and all the rest. We almost had to take the flight gear back when the first sergeant found out that none of us had actually been assigned to flight status, and could easily be told to do something else. But our enthusiasm must have counted for something, because we kept the gear and were assigned to helicopters in short order. We were officially gunners and assistant crew chiefs. None of us had ever fired a machine gun from the air, and we had had only one or two flights in any kind of helicopter.

The new gunners were piled into two H-21s and transported to a nearby ARVN (as the Army of Viet Nam was always referred to) rifle range to learn the basics of helicopter gunners—something not covered at the time at Fort Rucker's Army Aviation Center. The two aircraft flew a racetrack pattern past the targets while we each got our turn to fire, then we landed to see if anybody had hit anything. Our helicopter took off again for more of the same, and the other H-21 rolled over and thrashed itself to death. Although nobody was badly hurt, it was as much of a lesson as the machine gun instruction.

The 8th had been here for almost a year, and had seen a lot of action and had a fair number of losses, some to equipment failure, others to enemy action. By the time I arrived, the officers and enlisted soldiers had settled down to a routine; they knew the rules and the stakes of the game. They were combat veterans, tested by fire and blood, and the veterans taught and inspired the acolytes, as veterans always have. The 8th was a smooth-running combat operation, improvising like crazy, working hard, suffering with inadequate aircraft and supporting ARVN forces whose combat effectiveness was—well, shall we say—limited. But they had worked out the details of completing the mission they had been given, and they had done it under fire. They had been fighting and sometimes dying, unnoticed by the media and by the public. Now they were beginning to go home.

Although the American public didn't know what we were doing, the aviation community within the Army did. It was an exciting and innovative time for the Army, because aviation was being used in places and in ways never previously attempted, and important lessons were being learned and applied. In a primitive, tentative way, the Army was doing something of tremendous potential benefit. Of course most of us gunners thought little about it at the time; we were too busy and too young. It was simply exciting to be doing something real, far from the routines of safety and convention on the other side of the ocean. But I now know that our leaders were struggling with technical and tactical problems and inventing solutions that we aircrews carried out.

Over the next ten months I flew one hundred and twenty-seven combat missions all over the central part of Viet Nam—a fairly typical score for the time, but far fewer than the hundreds of sorties people would log later. Most were in H-21s, but two were with VNAF T-28s, the converted trainers used for close air support at the time. We carried rice and pigs and smelly Nuc Mam fish sauce into remote camps and to ARVN units in the field; we collected dead and wounded from landing zones (LZs) so small the rotor wash pushed the trees aside, allowing us to land. We carried frightened and bewildered refugees and sullen prisoners. Once we even carried a reporter.

But the best and the worst missions were the combat assaults against known VC positions, guaranteed to give an adrenaline rush that could last all day. The sheer pageantry of a major assault, with its parade of helicopters charging into genuine peril across the treetops at top speed, escorted by quick and agile fighters from the Vietnamese Air Force, was theater of the highest sort. Below us the landscape flashed. We cranked up our sensitivity as high as it would go—standing still, going fast, waiting for the moment when danger was revealed and the microsecond response was possible. It was an extremely intuitive problem, with absolutely no chance for contemplation or reasoned thought. There was no time to aim the machine gun; you had to play it as a natural extension of yourself, the way people play the piano after years of practice. Trees, paddies, empty fields rushed by in the sights of my machine gun. I will never forget the feel of the curvature of the trigger of that gun, the pulsing rhythm of the weapon when I turned it loose, the brilliant red of its tracers, and the way vegetation trembled under its blast. I also remember a small man in black running for a trench line; I fired at him until the gun hit the stops, a long, steady, careful, angry burst. The tracers danced out to him, and dust flew up around him, but he kept running, untouched. That's the way it was for many of us on both sides; we came back with a bullet hole in the engine compartment that day, but no damage other than to the sheet metal. Lots of other crews were not so blessed.

It was a kind of Terry and the Pirates era, and that made me an apprentice pirate, junior grade. It was great fun for a while; then it got scary in a pattern I later discovered was common. I saw too many dead helicopters, heard too many bullets crack past my door, lost too many of the guys I went to school with to stay comfortable and complacent. Part of the problem was the H-21, a gutless beast. On my first combat mission, my helicopter, loaded with ARVN troopers, didn't have enough power to clear the trees at the edge of the LZ, and our aft rotor blades had holes punched in them by the tree limbs. We staggered out of the LZ, vibrated to a secure spot, put tape over the holes, and then wobbled home. Mechanical problems caused us tremendous losses, far more than enemy action. During my tour I rode down one total engine failure and was aboard for many partial failures that demanded emergency landings. The H-21 was an accident looking for a place to happen.

It was with some surprise that I went home in one chunk, in 1963, to a country that still wasn't sure where Viet Nam was, much less that Americans were fighting there. We had been, I was told, "advisers," and our combat experience during that early period is still generally unknown.

My next assignment was to a school on the new CH-47A Chinook helicopter, and then to the experimental 11th Air Assault Division (AAD) at Fort Benning, Georgia. The early experiments with airmobility in Viet Nam were expanded to a huge test using the 11th AAD, and it was again my fortune to be a part of a pivotal action at a crucial time. My commander, Maj. Howard Porter, encouraged me to either go to Officer Candidate School or get out of the Army and into college. I got out in 1965, just as the 11th was converted to the 1st Cavalry Division (Airmobile) and deployed to An Khe near my old base at Qui Nhon. My company, I later learned, had suffered great losses in the battles that followed, and many of my friends were killed or wounded. They've always been in my thoughts, and never more than now, as I describe our military heirs and disciples.

As I write this it occurs to me that it is twenty-five years to the day that we flew an assault into the mountains west of Tuy Hoa, into a beehive. Chief Warrant Officer Holloway took a bullet through the head; the young officer in the left seat, who was on his first mission, had to fly back without the help of the instructor pilot (IP) who was teaching him the ropes. The helicopter was full of holes; gas poured from many hits on the fuel tank—this was just before the era of self-healing tanks—and the crew chief used his gloves to plug some of the holes. Still, fuel streamed out onto the floor and ran out into the slipstream, spraying past the hot exhaust. The new pilot managed to get the aircraft back to Tuy Hoa, and back on the ground, although Holloway was already dead. His blood covered the floor and had coated the underside of the helicopter like bright red paint. It was three days before Christmas.

I drop by The Wall when I'm in Washington and say "hi" to Holloway. His name is with those of the guys who died early. He wasn't the first, and he wasn't the last, and a lot of my friends joined him in the years to come. While I'm sad that they died, I'm glad that there were—and still are—people willing to risk their lives in the service of our national institutions and traditions. I don't think their deaths were in vain. They didn't attempt to be noble, but what they were sent to do was noble just the same.

Modern Army aviation is based to a large extent on the lessons we learned back then, during those first years in Viet Nam and in the 1964 trials of the 11th AAD. After recent visits to Forts Rucker, Benning, Hood, and Ord, I must say that many things have not changed in fundamental ways in all these years. Even my old Chinook is still alive and well, soldiering faithfully wherever the Army goes, although the new and improved D model no longer leaks hydraulic fluid the way my old A model did. But there are some changes, both in technology and in mission, that make Army aviation a significant player in the great game of war. The attack helicopter, represented in 1963 by a Huey carrying machine guns and rockets, has come a long way in the form of the Apache. The Army now uses aviation in a very bold way, and it is a real pleasure to see how capable the new systems and people are.

It's an honor to tell the story of Army aviation today, and a delight to see how much and how little have changed over the twenty-five years since we tested the new wings of combat operations.

There is still a spirit of commitment to mission, a kind of bright-eyed professionalism and dedication that I remember vividly—a quality I think is unique to Army aviation. And it is also wonderful to see how much improved the aircraft are, with power, armor, and technological additions none of us imagined.

The institution of the U.S. Army is loaded with traditions, one of which is that old soldiers always say that the *old* Army was the *good* Army, that things were tougher, better, more virtuous "way back when." You won't hear that from me. The people in Army aviation today are more intelligent and professional than ever, the missions are more realistic, training is far more intense and appropriate, and the systems available to fight with are far more capable and reliable than before. I've seen both. As an old soldier I am glad to say, these are the good old days.

Assault under fire, Viet Nam 1963.

Introduction:
Battle Position 41

It is nighttime in Central Germany. A snow falls in occasional flurries from a three-hundred-foot ceiling, but it is early winter and none has accumulated on the frozen ground. Dispersed beneath a stand of trees are several tents and vehicles, draped with camouflage netting: a tactical operations center (TOC) for an Army attack helicopter company. The only aid to navigation for someone seeking this little refuge is several green Chem-lights to guide the way through the gap in the razor wire and between the two nervous soldiers with Ml6s. Several figures move in pairs through the gloom, provide the correct response to the sentry's challenge, and slip carefully into the largest tent.

Although it is midnight, the sky to the east is already aglow . . . but not from an early sunrise. And the clouds overhead are not the source of the rumbling thunder that shakes the ground. Fifty kilometers to the east, the Soviet State Orchestra is playing its famous theme song, a powerful composition based on its large percussion section, played by battery-powered tubular instruments: hundreds of howitzers and artillery of 122mm and 152mm guns, and rockets and missiles of every tone and pitch. If they fall on you, they make a variety of cracks, bangs, and screeches. But from this distance, the effect is a kind of monotonous rumble, the same deep, flat note played over and over without rhythm, and the only damage they create is to the resolve of those who will have to stand up to them. The curtain has just risen on World War III.

AH-64 Apaches in low-level flight over the vast expanses of scrubland at Fort Hood, Texas. *George Hall photo.*

Inside the tent are small folding stools, a sheet metal stove, and a map board. A Coleman lantern illuminates the scene. Eighteen serious men are present, seventeen sitting, one standing before the board. Twelve are crews for the AH-64 Apache attack helicopters parked nearby, the rest are crews of OH-58 Kiowa scouts. All are in flight suits and survival vests, with helmet bags and map cases; and they are here to receive their first operation order in a very new war. The pilot standing is the commander of Bravo Company, 1st Battalion, 3d Aviation. The commander is a tall captain of thirty, an Airborne Ranger, much younger than many of those he will lead into battle; nonetheless, they call him "sir" on the ground, and "Gremlin Six" in the air. He begins:

"Let's get started," the Six says. "Roll call: Guns?"

"Up!" reports one of the pilots from the attack helicopter section.

"Scouts?"

"Up!" is the prompt reply.

Okay, pay attention. Hold your questions till I'm finished. Post your graphics at the end of the order. You all have a map and a commo/route card; time zone is local; company organization is SOP.

SITUATION — ENEMY . . . the anticipated invasion of Western Europe by Warsaw Pact forces was initiated four hours ago. The Soviet Eight Combined Arms Army is part of the first echelon. It is composed of the 39th Guards Motorized Rifle Division, the 9th Guards Tank Division, and the 120th Guards Motorized Rifle Division. The 4th Guards Motorized Rifle Division and the 79th Tank Division are currently twenty to twenty-five kilometers behind the 8th Combined Arms Army in echelon. The Combined Arms Army frontage is

The eyes of Army aviation, the multitalented OH-58 Delta model, sporting its million dollar "beachball." The Kiowa observation helicopter can spot and designate targets many miles away through dark, rain, fog, then hand them off to artillery, Air Force fighters, Army attack helicopters, or even ground units.

approximately fifty kilometers.

Our 11th Armored Cavalry Regiment has attrited the first echelon to approximately 50 percent combat effectiveness. They are currently conducting a passage of lines.

The division G-2 has concentrated efforts on several NAI [named areas of interest] on the key avenues of approach into the division sector. The 79th Guards Tank Division should be employed in our sector in a continued effort to establish a foothold or penetration, which they have thus far

been unable to achieve. The division commander needs time to completely attrit the first echelon; therefore, he is going to employ our battalion against the 79th Guards Tank Division.

Enemy morale is currently high. They have T-72 and T-80 tanks plus their normal organic

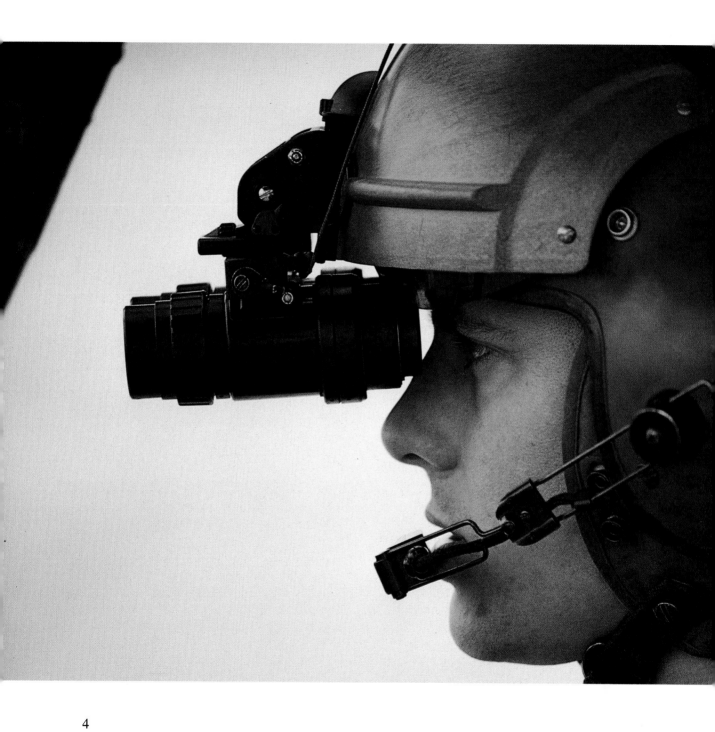

complement of air defense and field artillery. Their recent action was an attack through the Eigerfeld Bowl, where they were engaged by the 11th Armored Cavalry Regiment conducting a covering force battle forward of the division.

Enemy likely courses of action: a continued effort to break through to Frankfort. NBC [nuclear, biological, chemical warfare] has not been employed as of yet. They have been using a lot of EW [electronic warfare].

Our division's mission is to defend, attrit, and destroy the 8th Combined Arms Army as they move into sector. The Aviation Brigade and Battalion mission: our battalion will be employed against the 79th Guards Tank Division at 0520 this morning in Engagement Area [EA] RED. Alpha, Bravo, and Charlie companies will be employed.

Weather and light: Ceiling is expected to rise to 2,000 feet, visibility between one and two miles. Sunrise will be at 0720; sunset at 1750.

Mission: Bravo Company "Gremlins" will attack to destroy lead regiments of the 79th Guards Tank Division no later than 0520 into EA RED.

Concept of the operation: To completely destroy the first echelon regiments, not letting them penetrate farther than the north-south autobahn shown on the graphic, and to slow the 79th Guards employment with the 1st of the 3d.

Gremlin Six works through the briefing format, and all the crews scribble frantically, copying down illumination data, frequencies, call

---

OH-58 pilot sports the latest thing in fashion eyewear for evenings out, the amazing AN/PVS-7 night vision goggles. Even starlight through clouds is enough for these things to work, revealing a detailed world on the darkest night.

signs, checkpoints, passage point location, times in and out of the engagement area, fire support, and the SEAD (suppression of enemy air defenses) plan. The known enemy locations are copied carefully from the map, even though nobody expects the enemy to stay put. The Gremlins will have some fire support from an artillery battery, but no air cover.

Gremlin Six continues:

"Scouts, you'll open and close the passage points; you'll be the first in and clear the routes. You'll also call the artillery for the SEAD and be my relay back to battalion headquarters."

A barrage of data is absorbed by the crews, all of which focuses on a small circle drawn on the map. Labeled BP 41, this circle is just one of many possible battle positions the S-3 shop has defined, but it is the only one that will be used. On the ground it is just a hillside, about a thousand meters across. On the other side of the hill is a valley, with pastures, a few houses, several roads—and the advance units of 79th Guards Tank Division, moving west. On the overlay in the Gremlin TOC, the valley is enclosed by another circle and labeled EA RED, just one of many possible engagement areas but the one that has been selected by the fates and fortunes of war—along with the S-3.

Gremlin Six finishes his briefing and asks for questions. There are none.

The pilots file out of the TOC and through the wire, past the sentries and off to their helicopters, dispersed nearby in a large pasture. The ground crews have fueled and armed the helicopters with a full load, and they are ready to fly. On the inboard wing stations of each are eight Hellfire missiles, each easily capable of killing a main battle tank at a range of four miles. The outboard pylons hold rockets—there are thirty-eight on each aircraft, most with multipurpose submunitions; there are also four warheads with thousands of tiny steel arrows the crews call "nails." Under the chin of the helicopter is the 30mm chain gun, ready and waiting with 1,200 rounds of ammunition.

There are thirty minutes left till crank time, and they are busy ones; the crews mount their chargers and work through the prestart checklist in the chill. Gunners begin entering Doppler navigation data, target coordinates, laser code data, and radio frequencies. Commo checks are made, on both secure and unscrambled systems. The TADS (target acquisition and designation system) is checked, along with the jammers. The auxiliary power units are lit off, and the generators come on line; the birds come alive, pulsing with nervous energy and electrical power. At precisely 0445 the engine start sequence is engaged on nine helicopters in the pasture, and fifteen others nearby. In a few minutes rotors are turning, and at five minutes before the hour the helicopters pull pitch, rise away from the ground, and are gone.

Despite the darkness and the rain, Gremlin flight skims the trees at 110 knots. Without any visible landmark or guide outside the cockpit, the crews all know exactly where they are, exactly where they are going, and exactly how they will zigzag across the battlefield to the target. In front of each pilot and gunner is a small screen with a clear (although green) view of the world outside; this little vision also displays computer navigation data and all the weapons information required to deliver the missiles and rockets and bullets with precision—even in the dark.

The screens show a cold landscape, but the FLIR (forward-looking infrared) display reveals

scattered hot spots where our armor awaits the onslaught. The armor units have been warned, but still the "passage of lines" remains a major hazard for a cross FLOT mission. Closer to the FEBA (forward edge of battle area), the fires of burning vehicles become a useful source of illumination for the night vision devices, bouncing off the cloud cover and adding enough light for an even better view.

The OH-58 Kiowa, known to the company as Gremlin One-Two, breaks off at the passage

If this OH-58 wasn't posing nicely for the camera, all you'd see was the beachball peeking through the trees. From a few hundred meters away the helicopter becomes practically invisible while providing targets and information to the rest of the team.

point, to hold the door open for our return.

Gremlin Three-Zero leads the light section. The pilot is a warrant officer who has been flying "guns" since he joined the Army in 1967 and is now in his forties. His front seater is young enough to be his son, but they're a team, within a series of teams. As they blast through the hostile

A daylight TV view on the multifaceted display of an OH-58 ready for takeoff. The CH-47 is over on the other side of the ramp and is not usually a target.

An AH-64 Apache comes ripping along in "nap-of-the-earth" flight, out of sight (the driver hopes) of the forces of evil. At night, thermal and low-light vision devices permit this kind of navigation with fairly high speed and reasonable safety.

night, no tracers greet them, no warnings of gun control radars paint them with evil intent. They run in toward the target just as planned, using the rolling terrain for cover and concealment with the skill of a fabled Apache, slowing as they approach the release point. The APR 39 radar warning system chirps and strobes intermittently now, an indication that the antiaircraft weapons systems that guard Soviet armor are awake and at work. Although our crews can pick up the enemy's emissions, they can't possibly identify us down here in the clutter. The Apaches will remain masked, firing their rockets "indirect fire." The enemy will never know what hit them, let alone where it came from.

"Release point. MPSM," the Gremlins hear on the radio. Our crews will use the multipurpose

submunition warheads first, as planned. The computer display continues to tell each crew where they are in the inky, hostile night, and where the target is in relation to them. Now, as they come into effective range for the rockets, it also provides much of the engagement calculations and will put the rockets where they will do the most good—or damage.

"Kevin, co-op rockets," Gremlin Three-Zero tells his front seater over the internal communication system (ICS). The flight continues toward Battle Position 41, but won't wait to fight.

"Roger, slaved to target; range set."

"MPSM zoned—we're set," Three-Zero tells Six. The other three tell him the same thing.

"MPSM—NOW!"

All the Apaches unload their rockets on the

Soviet vehicles and armor while they refuel and rearm. Each helicopter fires thirty-two rockets in less than half a second; they slither out of their tubes, one after another a few milliseconds apart, each trailing a brilliant white path of light for an instant. The computer has combined range and position data, set the fuses in the rockets, and elevated the launchers so the rockets will dispense the submunitions at a precise altitude over the target rather than on top of it.

Within only a few heartbeats, the first rocket arrives and pops, and nine little cylinders float down under small parachutes. The cylinders are only about three inches across, but each contains a shaped charge that can cut through the vulnerable top armor of almost any tank and certainly any lighter vehicle they land on. But the cylinders will also spray shrapnel for a considerable radius when they land on bare ground, and the shrapnel is deadly to things like fuel trucks, antiaircraft

An Apache cuts loose two Hydra 70 arrows with multipurpose submunition warheads. The warheads will dispense more than a dozen armor-killing charges over a target, condemning both vehicles and personnel on the ground.

That's an M88 tank recovery vehicle under the crosshairs of an Apache's portable TV. Even though the M88 is over a mile away it is an easy target; a press of a button will "box" it and lock the computer-driven sight on its armored bulk.

gerous to both the hunted and the hunter. Battle Position 41 is about six kilometers from the target—a little less than four miles. Distance protects against the deadly accurate tank main gun, which is reliable to about two klicks, but the distance only helps the enemy missiles.

Gremlin flight slips into BP 41, protected by a low hill. "Coming up," Gremlin Six calls, and all five rise until their vision over the trees is clear. What they see is amazing—dozens of vehicles burn and secondary explosions pop all over the target, an oasis of light in a desert of gloom. But appearances can be deceiving; the most dangerous and valuable enemy assets are the most likely to have survived. Now is the time to engage them, and to risk engagement in turn.

All the crews study the target area with a wide field of view on the TADS display in the cockpit. Gremlin Six will put his laser on the center of the target area, indicating the center of the pie that the five crews will share. Each will be responsible for killing anything remaining in its sector.

"From the spot—heavy section left, light section right!" calls the Six. The crews will stick with the SOP that says that the "heavy" section of the flight (the "Six" and the other two AH-64s) will shoot at targets to the left of the position marked with the laser—the "spot" they all see on their screens. The light section with two aircraft gets the targets on the right.

Through the smoke and snow the tanks stand out clearly in the thermal sights, and there is a bright dot glowing prominently in the center of the confusion. This is the reference point for the Gremlins, and now each crew starts to work on its slice of the target, sights at high magnification now.

Gremlin Three-Zero's front seater pushes his

missiles, and the soldiers who use them. Fifteen helicopters, each shooting thirty-two rockets containing nine bomblets apiece, equal 4,320 submunitions to saturate the target area. It erupts in flashes and smoke, and then the secondary explosions begin. The law of averages condemns many of the vehicles and most of the people in the area they thought was safe and secure. Tanks catch fire, tanks explode, fuel tankers add heat and light to the scene, and an occasional surface-to-air missile cooks off and flops around like an angry, fire-breathing fish. From the point of view of someone on the target, the effect is the same as four thousand 105mm artillery rounds arriving on the same spot within a few seconds of each other. It is devastating.

But there is more to come, and it is more dan-

The helmet-mounted display (HMD) is just a tiny TV screen whose image is reflected from the monocle. But it gets some great programs: flight information, targeting data, and a bright view of the terrain in the middle of the night.

Capt. Rick Rife, Gremlin Six. His HMD gets its information from those sensors on the nose: laser rangefinder/designator for straight shooting, daylight TV for target acquisition, and a thermal imager for night flight and firing.

ICS button without thinking about it: "I've got targets!"

"APR strobes at ten, twelve, and two o'clock; possible SA-8 and 'zoos!'" This is the warning of active air defenses, including surface-to-air missiles and the rapid fire ZSU-23 cannon. But there isn't much the gunner can do about it now except to reply, "Looking."

"Jammer active!" the pilot calls. It's time to get to work.

"I've got a 13, tracking," the gunner reports as he prepares to fire at one of the survivors, a SA-13 air defense system. His head is down, and he steers the cross hairs on his screen until they are centered on a glowing mass that represents a tracked vehicle mounting four large missiles. The pilot monitors the Hellfire missile systems, all

eight of which are alive and well and ready to fly. Each has a laser seeker in its nose, and will fly a preprogrammed course that will bring down its wrath on top of anything in range that happens to reflect a particularly coded laser light.

"In constraints!" the gunner hears, meaning his missile is good to go. With a flash, the Hellfire dashes off into the night. "Missile out. Laser on," the gunner reports, keeping the sight aligned. With a press of a button on his left handgrip, he forms a box around the target and locks the sight onto the target, leaving himself the uncertain luxury of monitoring his systems for the twenty seconds it will take the Hellfire to arrive. In back the APR flashes and chirps its message of possible doom, but it isn't indicating that Three-Zero is being tracked . . . yet.

After making a terrible mess downrange with gunfire and rockets, an Apache from the 82d Airborne Division beats a hasty retreat.

A new ball of fire erupts on the far side of the target, then seems to evaporate in a flash of white light as secondary explosions vaporize Three-Zero's first victim. "Missile impact," the gunner reports. It is the very first Hellfire he has ever shot. The pilot quickly drops the Apache below the tree line, repositions several hundred meters to the right, and comes up again.

"Missile out on a T-80," is the call. Bright green balls of light float through the sky in the general direction of Gremlin Three-Zero, tracers from small-caliber automatic weapons—a distraction but not yet a real danger. There are fifteen Hellfires in flight, each seeking the foundations of the Soviet assault, the sharp, armored edge of a division. One by one they come crashing down on the thin armored roofs of T-80s and

T-72s, on ZSUs and SA-8s, chipping away at the combat power of the Red Horde. But the party is far from over, and the enemy isn't ready to roll over and play dead. Gremlin Three-Zero's APR screen is lit up like a Christmas tree, showing the strength and bearings on threat radars that are painting them in search mode. Now one of the strobes shows a system that has gone active and has begun tracking them. The jammer isn't throwing it off.

"Kevin—I think they've got a lock on us."

The gunner is busy. "Three seconds to impact . . . "

The APR display suddenly brightens. "Roger. Shit! Missile launch, two o'clock!"

" . . . Impact. Kill. Looking . . . "

"I'm chaffing! Down and right!" the pilot calls, preparing to dance away from the threat.

"Clear!" the front seater replies, and down they go, sliding sideways at forty-five knots. The pilot punches his chaff button twice, and a cloud of aluminum foil bursts by the tail rotor and disperses into a large radar reflector that is intended to deceive the missile guidance system. It works. A fireball envelops the airspace that Gremlin Three-Zero had occupied seconds before. Now the hunter becomes the hunted as Three-Zero looks for the source of the scare.

"Coming up," is the call as the helicopter unmasks again. The APR strobe provides a perfect bearing for the gunner. "Roger, looking . . . got him! SA-8; missile out!" Another Hellfire slides off into the night. "He's looking far left." The SA-8 fires at Alpha Company.

"MISSILE, MISSILE, MISSILE!" someone yells on the battalion net and the threat blows up inside a cloud of chaff.

"MAYDAY! I'm hit—number one engine out!"

comes from Charlie Company, adding to the rising traffic on the radio.

"Impact. Kill on the SA-8," the young gunner reports to his back seater. There are still targets: "Missile out on a T-80." This is his fifth; three left. The APR is silent and dark; the enemy radars are either dead or pretending to be. He sees another tank near the first, and without waiting for number five to hit cuts loose number six: "Missile number six out . . . impact on five . . . kill! New target: T-80."

"Kevin, I've got movement at ten o'clock high, two spots." There is something in the air out there, headed this way.

"Roger. Impact on six . . . kill! Looking." The gunner strains to see the new threat.

"Gunner! Target!"

"Roger, slaving," he replies, switching his display to duplicate the pilot's. "Got it! Looks like Hinds, inbound—four at least."

"GREMLINS, HINDS, TEN O'CLOCK HIGH, ENGAGING!" the pilot calls over the battalion net.

"Range good, missile out, tracking good," reports the gunner as the seventh Hellfire departs on its mission. One of the enemy helicopters disappears in a flash as another launches one of its AT-6 missiles at the attackers.

Gremlin Three-Zero's pilot has been saving six rockets for just this occasion: the crews call them "nails" because all they carry for a warhead are little steel arrows that look like thin two-inch nails. But there are 2,500 in each rocket, and when the warhead bursts open they form a cloud of sharp-pointed high-velocity needles that is 35 meters across moving at 2,500 feet per second. One of the Hinds flies into this cloud and is penetrated in hundreds of places. The Soviet crewmen are hit by dozens of the nails and immediately forget the AT-6 missile they've been guiding; their helicopter pitches up abruptly and continues to attempt to perform a loop, but instead staggers over on one side and flies inverted into the ground, exploding in another fireball.

Another fireball explodes nearby and a quick glance reveals an Apache from Charlie Company going down in minimal control.

"New target—missile out! Last missile in the air."

"Roger."

"Damn! Lost the target in the flames . . . lost lock. There he is! Impact! Secondary."

Over the battalion net the familiar voice of the commander says: "Gremlins, rally. More enemy air inbound, fifteen klicks." It's time to get the hell out of Dodge. Gremlin Six calls back to the Kiowa at the FLOT: "Gremlin One-Two, Gremlin Six. We're inbound."

"Roger, the gate will be open," the guard replies.

Blasting through the night across the treetops at 140 knots and 50 feet of altitude, the Gremlins rush back to the relative safety and security of friendly forces. The Six calls: "Status."

"Two-One, up."

"Two-Two is up."

"Two-Five has number one generator out, light damage left side—good otherwise."

"Three-Zero, up."

"Two-Zero, TADS has failed. We had a near miss and suspect shrapnel damage. We'll make it."

Later, back on the ground—at a new TOC and a new forward area rearm and refuel point (FARRP)—the Gremlins provide their BDA (bomb damage assessment). The MPSM from the five helicopters killed three ZSUs, two SA-8s, at least a dozen BMPs (armored fighting vehicles with a tank gun and missile but with thinner armor), and a like number of tanks. The crews lost count of the number of burning trucks and BTRs (light armored personnel carriers). Of the forty Hellfire missiles fired, kills were observed on one ZSU; two SA-13s; two SA-8s; and thirty T-64, T-72, and T-80 tanks. One Hind helicopter was also killed with a Hellfire. One more fell to the "nails." Two of the forty Hellfires missed and one malfunctioned.

Altogether, the battalion's helicopters have killed more than a hundred main battle tanks and at least as many other vehicles in a few minutes. The damage inflicted had a price tag, though: Alpha Company lost one helicopter and another was badly damaged. Charlie Company had moderate damage on two and light damage on another. It could have been much worse, and much better for the enemy, but a combination of luck, technology, planning, leadership, training, and audacity favored the Gremlins this time.

PUSH TO TEST

This scenario is largely true, although it is based on training exercises rather than bloodshed. The opening battles of World War III are fought on a nearly daily basis, with varying outcomes, by the people and the units from the friendly side who will have to fight them with real bullets. For now, the rockets and missiles are laser beams or displays in elaborate simulators, but there is genuine sweat and sometimes genuine fear, and sometimes there are even genuine casualties. The concept the Army applies is to make its preparation absolutely as realistic as possible, short of a shoot-out.

This scenario is true, too, in the minds of the people who plan, fund, and design the weapons systems, strategies, and tactics needed to defeat the threats to our political and cultural independence. This is the way it must happen if an invasion of Europe is ever to be defeated. The attack helicopter is one small part of a big game plan—an expensive and crucial part. It will have to work, along with all the other elements, when and if push ever comes to shove.

At this writing, the Soviet Union and its allies, and the United States and its allies, haven't elected to fight it out in Europe. It is starting to look like the fight might even be avoided. The threat has been great enough, for long enough, however, that tremendous national assets have been dedicated to the possibility that it might happen. Weapons have been designed and soldiers trained to be able to defeat such a massive attack. American soldiers train in the most realistic ways that can be conceived, and battles like this one

are an almost daily occurrence at the vast National Training Center in California, at the Joint Readiness Training Center (JRTC) in Arkansas, and all over the northeastern parts of Germany. And although the victory here went to the friendly forces, it is often the other way around.

Army aviation is just one part of the larger mission of the Army and the other armed forces. It is tremendously complicated, full of new technologies and exotic aircraft. It is also a very human endeavor, highly reliant on the intangible but essential qualities of individual people—both men and women—who operate and maintain the aircraft. Army aviation has a fascinating past, and an intriguing future. Army aviators have attack and "cavalry" missions, carry battalions of soldiers into battle, carry their heavy equipment and supplies to them, and observe the battlefield for the commander. All these missions fit into a basic doctrine called "AirLand Battle." I'll try to explain them all in the chapters that follow.

Over the hills and through the woods, a Kiowa on the move.

The Mission
of Army Aviation

W e can't talk about Army aviation without considering how it fits into the world of warfare, of which it is a tiny element. Army, Navy, Air Force, Marine, and Coast Guard organizations will all have to fight the next war together, just as they have in the past. From the point of view of the planners and the Joint Chiefs of Staff, the ultimate weapon isn't the stealth bomber or the nuclear weapon. It's the individual soldier, the guy the Army calls an Eleven Bravo, the uncommon foot soldier. He can be a Marine or a Ranger, or a member of any of the Army's infantry divisions, but the basic idea behind our armed forces is that he is the focus of everything. Army aviation exists to help these Eleven Bravos survive and prevail. The whole Army spends a lot of time thinking about how to make life easier and longer for these soldiers, and they've come up with a few key ideas that are important in understanding how Army aviation works.

The planners who try to anticipate what the next big war will be like have the job of integrating all the U.S. and friendly forces into the most economical and effective fighting force possible. Their doctrine is called AirLand Battle, and involves a close integration of the many Air Force, Navy, and Army commands. Army aviation fits into AirLand Battle in many ways; the antiarmor attack mission is only one. Army aviation will not win such a war alone, and the Apaches will not be the only heroes. There will be Air Force A-10s and F-16s overhead, Marines and Army infantry everywhere, tanks and artil-

Gremlin Three-Zero unmasks to fire at a suspicious photographer. Army tactics use cover and concealment rather than brute force or speed for protection against hostile fire, and a hillside is cheap, reliable armor.

lery slugging it out, and a tremendous logistic effort behind the FEBA.

The business of Army aviation is to be a reliable, effective, fully integrated kind of air force that a ground commander can call on right now to support his scheme of maneuver. It is related to the job the other Air Force is supposed to do. This has been a problem for as long as there has been an Air Force, a subject to be discussed in a following chapter.

THREE ROLES FOR AVIATION

Army aviation has three basic roles to play, and all are closely related to the missions of the ground Army within the formal doctrine known as AirLand Battle.

The first is known as *combat*: to attack major assets of the enemy, particularly armor, with its potential for rapid movement and potent firepower. This is the job of the attack helicopter AH-64 Apache, a complicated and capable system that generally lives and works with armored divisions and augments their missions. It is also the job of a kind of aerial cavalry that rides off over the hill to see what and who are out there. This is generally the job of the venerable AH-1 Cobra, in close cooperation with the observation helicopter OH-58 Kiowa, who together go off in search of adventure for all manner of infantry and armor organizations.

The second role is called *combat support*, the mission of moving large numbers of soldiers quickly into battle, the air assault job performed by the utility helicopter UH-60 Black Hawk.

And the last major mission, known either as

combat service support or "beans and bullets," is the job of that faithful Indian companion, the cargo helicopter CH-47 Chinook. It involves supporting all the diverse units that do the fighting by moving their artillery, ammunition, scout teams, food, fuel, casualties, and all the rest.

PRINCIPLES OF LAND COMBAT

The battalion structure Army wide includes a headquarters and three companies, about forty-five helicopters in strength. Three battalions are the foundation of a brigade, and three brigades make a division in the traditional design of army organizations. Aviation fits into the Army in lots of different ways, each with different talents and abilities. A special organization like the 101st Airborne Division (Air Assault) is designed and trained to do particular kinds of missions with an extraordinary skill and precision. When the 101st goes off to war, it takes along nearly four hundred helicopters: Cobras and Apaches for the attack role as well as for aeroscouting; Black Hawks and Chinooks for combat support missions, lifting troops into battle, and airmobility; Kiowas to watch the battlefield and report targets and correct artillery; and three dozen Hueys to help with medevacs and command and control. There are even dedicated "quick fix" Black Hawks for electronic warfare missions.

Together, these helicopters perform the same kinds of tactical support in the air that tanks, armored personnel carriers, trucks, and resupply vehicles do on the ground. And they bring to AirLand Battle an expansion of the combat power a commander can apply.

The Army has a basic plan for fighting the next major conflict, and it applies to minor conflicts as well. Every person and system described in this book has a role to play in this plan, and neither the systems nor the people make a lot of sense if you don't have a basic understanding of the rules of the game.

AirLand Battle has four basic tenets: initiative, agility, depth, and synchronization.

Initiative means that everybody is expected to look for opportunities to score points, be aggressive, and take intelligent chances. American soldiers traditionally use their orders and plans as advisories, not commandments. (A Soviet general once said that Americans write great orders and never read them; a German general during World War II remarked after his capture that he wasn't fighting against an army but against a kind of chaos.) Unlike almost all other armies, and particularly those of the Warsaw Pact, individual soldiers are trusted to use their individual initiative to further the basic plans they've been given.

Agility means the ability to move combat power quickly from one place to another. One rifleman—from a task force commander's point of view—represents the minimum amount of combat power. But if you take, for example, a battalion of Rangers and deliver them suddenly to an enemy headquarters far behind the lines, you can make a big difference in the flow of the fight. Sometimes that kind of agility can be accomplished on foot, sometimes with armor, sometimes with aviation. Agility is the ability to act first, and is required for initiative. It lets a commander apply strength against weakness. Aviation permits a commander to move his combat power quickly, to concentrate it where it will do the most good—or harm—at the least cost.

The OV-1 Mohawk has been part of Army aviation since the early '60s, performing a critical mission for the force—gathering highly detailed information with special cameras and radar. The Mohawk is the only aircraft in the Army inventory with an ejection seat. It has a crew of two, a pilot and an enlisted sensor operator.

Depth refers to the intention to fight across a wide area, without a sharp line between friendly forces and the enemy. American planners expect units to be cut off sometimes, to be surrounded and still function. Depth means that once combat is joined, the enemy will never be safe anywhere. During World War II both the Germans and the Japanese believed that their home countries could be insulated from battle, but Army aviation took the fight to them and eventually devastated the urban areas of both nations. Americans have developed the concept of the raid to a minor art form.

Army air permits a commander to use initiative to attack an enemy constantly and everywhere that can hurt him: Apaches and Cobras can strike deep or chew on the flanks; the Kiowa can use its laser to designate many targets for precision-guided munitions; the Black Hawk and Chinook can deliver battalions of infantry and batteries of artillery to bring combat power to bear quickly on an enemy.

Synchronization means that everybody plays the same tune off the same sheet of music. It means that everybody's efforts are coordinated and focus on the same objective. If some junior leader wants to take the initiative because he sees

a chance to make a big dent, he should first make sure he's in sync with the basic plan and not playing cowboy.

These four basic tenets are the foundation for the way the Army does business, and for the way Army aviation fits into the fight. They are practiced, consciously and otherwise, worldwide,

Interior view of the EH-60. This version of the Black Hawk is tricked out with a highly sophisticated system for intercepting (*left side*) and jamming (*right side*) enemy communications. The EH-60 is just one of the many ways the Army uses aviation to accomplish its AirLand Battle missions.

with blanks and real bullets, day and night, every day.

THE ARMY AVIATION CENTER

It takes anywhere from about six months to a year to qualify to thrash around the sky in Army green and get paid for it. The junior enlisted crew go through a sequence of schools designed for specific aircraft, and it will be their job to attend Black Hawks, Kiowas, Chinooks, and the rest. The enlisted ranks also include a lot of essential folks who don't routinely fly, but without their efforts nobody else would either. They labor long and hard to keep the Apaches and Cobras healthy and ready for hunting season.

Most Army aviators are warrant officers, those specialist soldiers whose rank is somewhere in the nether land between commissioned officer and senior NCO. A regular officer's career requires a tremendous variety of experience and ability. A warrant does one thing for a whole career, does it well, and does little else. At Fort Rucker he learns to fly a helicopter.

One of the grand traditions of the Army is to stash its installations in remote corners of the universe, so the Army Aviation Center is in a rural corner of Alabama far from the distractions of big cities and their expensive real estate.

There's a lot to do at Fort Rucker, Alabama. There's a great museum, full of airplanes. There's a department store right outside the gate, selling aviation supplies only. There are sights to see, if you like looking at helicopters. There are restaurants, if you like barbecue or Big Macs. The local bookstore features books about military aviation. Yep, Fort Rucker is a cultural delight!

The isolation is probably a good idea, because the several thousand students who come here every year to become warrant officers and pilots don't need anything else to think about. Most will spend about a year here, learning basics and fine points. Rucker has the busiest aviation companies in the Army, with many of the best aviators serving as instructors. A very high proportion wear combat patches on their right shoulders, a not-so-subtle proclamation of graduation from a different kind of school.

Simulation has become a major part of the training for all soldiers, and some of the best systems are available for aviators. Fort Rucker and many other installations have large and expensive flight simulators that permit pilots and gunners to do all sorts of things that they hope will never happen in the real world, like engine fires at awkward moments, or difficult combinations of load, altitude, wind, temperature, and mission that are guaranteed to crunch the airplane. But in the simulator you can walk away from the crash, probably taking some lessons with you.

The simulators are very convincing, and still photographs of the terrain imagery give little sense of the overall effect. You sit in a helicopter cockpit—an AH-1 Cobra for example—which is mounted in a big black box. Three television screen images—one in front of you and one on either side—pretty well cover your field of vision. Before the technician fires up the system, it seems

---

Warrant officer candidates march off to class at Fort Rucker, Alabama. They will spend about a year here, learning to stand up straight, memorizing silly songs, and will in the process become extraordinarily proficient helicopter pilots.

just like a television—a graphics vision of an airport runway, obviously a kind of low grade cartoon. Terrain features are rather coarse and objects are not highly detailed, but then things start to happen. Your engine is suddenly running and the rotors flicker overhead. Pull up on the collective and you hear the engine respond and feel the airframe resonate as the power increases. The image out the cockpit shifts slightly as your helicopter gets light on the skids; and as you come up to a hover, you are no longer in a fantasy,

but in a world where real things will happen if you don't mind your manners. The technician suddenly adds a thirty-knot tail wind across the ramp, and you'd better be very careful with your hover technique. In the image on the other side of the canopy are triangular pine trees, stark and simple buildings, and hard-edged hills and mountains. If you clip one of those trees with your tail rotor, you'll get a look at the last second or so of your life before the screen freezes; the sweat on your palms will be real.

The people who operate the simulator work with the pilots to develop the skills the pilot wants to improve. Do you and your gunner need to polish your TOW missile skills? No problem, you can go head to head with the most sophisticated and capable tanks, light armor, air defense, and electronic countermeasure (ECM) assets the Soviets have to offer. If you two are a new team, the operators will be nice at first: the threats may hold still and not shoot back while you shoot at them. Then, after you've killed a bunch of them, they'll start moving around and shooting back. A Hind helicopter might pop up and launch a Sagger missile at you, and you'd better know what to do or you'll "get your clock cleaned," as they say.

Going one on one with an enemy system is one thing, but when the technician thinks you guys are pretty sharp, he'll start adding threats and you will find yourself in a worst-case-scenario nightmare as tanks, missiles, small arms, and enemy air all decide to use you for target practice. And it isn't a game, either. Crews come out of the black box screaming at each other. "YOU ALMOST GOT US KILLED OUT THERE!" seems to be a popular line. Other fliers throw up.

If your profession is to be the quickest gun or the straightest shooter, you want all the practice you can get, under the most difficult conditions, against the best the opposition can offer. The TOW and Hellfire missiles cost too much to fire on other than high holy days, except in the simulator, where they cost about a dime each. The facility at Rucker opens at 0600 and closes at

Down in the treetops is where the lessons of the simulator pay off. A Cobra on a scouting trip hides behind a hill before popping up to see what's on the other side.

2200, and is usually booked solid, with a waiting list of volunteers in case somebody doesn't show.

When the students leave Fort Rucker for the real world, they will become members of very different kinds of units. They will not join aloof aviation units as in the past, but will join aviation battalions, brigades, or regiments that are part and parcel of larger traditional ground organizations. They will go to the 3d Armored Cavalry Regiment, the 7th Infantry Division (Light), the 101st Airborne (Air Assault), or any of dozens of other "parent commands." Then they will learn to fly in support of the tanks and the troopers, of the artillery and engineers in all the environments for which the Army trains—jungle, desert, mountains, urban, hot, and cold—in training exercises

and perhaps in real combat. They will continue to train and prepare themselves for as long as they wear the sage green flight suit of an Army aviator, because training is the work of the peacetime Army. The odds are good that sometime in a career of thirty years, their services may be needed somewhere out in the real world, and then the learning curve will become steeper, and an entirely different set of lessons will be added to the ones of peacetime. The rewards of Army aviation are quite different from those of the other services, but they are significant just the same. And if push comes to shove again, as it always seems to, Army aviation will be playing a more important role than ever before.

HOW TO FLY A HELICOPTER

The jet jockeys of the Air Force and the Navy have been hogging the glory for entirely too long, but do they deserve it? Enquiring minds want to know! The Army style of doing things, you may have noticed, is with helicopters, flown for the most part as close to the trees as you can get without pruning them. Other branches of military aviation think this approach is dumber than a box of rocks, and will be happy to tell you so. The United States Air Force and Navy and Marines tend to think that the only place to do good is far, far up in the sky, preferably several miles from

A battalion of Army aviators pose formally at Fort Hood, Texas. *George Hall photo.*

the ground with all its tacky people and their petty problems. Far, too, from the battle, say Army aviators.

Since the jet jockeys get so much press and glamor and feature film fantasies like *Top Gun*, why don't we consider the problem of tactical aviation from the point of view of the only aviators who actually make a difference, the helo drivers of the Army? If you offer to buy them a drink, they will gladly supply you with a full set of highly classified information that the forces of evil would probably kill for. Get out your notebook and pay close attention, because this is the straight stuff.

Okay, we'll start by revealing some unofficial U.S. Army secrets, beginning by telling you that almost everything you've heard about fighter airplanes is a lie. First, any idiot can get a fixed-wing high-performance jet into the air. That's right, even *you* can get an F-15, F/A-18, or SR-71 up into the sky, as long as somebody will loan you the keys. The only hard part will be getting it started and away from the hangar.

If you can steer a kiddie car, you can taxi any fixed-wing airplane of any size, from a little Cessna to a B-52, and if you can get to the end of the runway, you can get it off the ground. For the little guys like the F-18s, it's all done with toe brakes. Want to turn right? Step on the right pedal's toe brake. By using the brakes alone, you trundle down the taxiway to the end of a long strip of concrete, which Air Force and Navy student pilots learn is called a "runway." There is a dotted line down the middle so the jet drivers know which side they're supposed to use.

Once you make sure you're pointing in the right direction, all you have to do is push the throttles all the way forward, sit back and relax, and watch the world go by. As long as you keep the wheels on the concrete, you'll go faster and faster until, at about 120 knots indicated airspeed, you can put a little back pressure on the stick—not much, just a little. The plane will feel light, the nose will come up, and then all three wheels are off and you are airborne. All U.S. Army aviators could do this much when they were five years old, some earlier.

Once airborne, though, every jet driver has two large problems, the first of which is finding something useful to do with his airplane. Almost all Air Force, Navy, and Marine "fast movers" are supposed to get far up in the sky and then shoot down members of the opposing team with "fire-and-forget" missiles. This is supposed to achieve something called "air superiority" when there is no other team left. Air superiority was achieved over North and South Viet Nam for almost every second of the ten years we were busy there, and of course it made a tremendous difference in the outcome! The other thing jet drivers do is drop large quantities of explosives, the usual result of which is to make loud noises and holes in the ground that will later fill up with rainwater. Neither of these things has much effect on most battles. Occasionally, a stray bomb will fall on a genuine military target and actually help us win the AirLand Battle, but not often.

Although jet drivers brag about how fast their planes will go, they don't tell you the whole truth. First, they've got to go fast or they fall right out of the sky and make a big mess; those puny little wings don't work well without a lot of air going by. Second, the process of going fast (to stay in the air) prevents them from doing anything worthwhile to help the fight on the ground, which is the only fight that really matters. Third, although they may fly very fast indeed, they tend to do it far from the earth, so the sensation is about as exciting as driving fifty-five miles an hour on the freeway: the ground slowly slides astern far below, out of sight and mind.

The USAF and Navy fighter pilots are afraid that if they come close to the ground, they might hit something or people might shoot at them, so they try to stay way up in the sky until the war's over. On those special occasions when they do come back down to earth and try to defeat the forces of evil, that speed makes it difficult for them to see or hit anything of significance. You simply can't see, much less put ordnance on a point target when it's jamming past your window at a thousand miles an hour and fifty feet below, unless you've got lots of expensive help. Even so, jet drivers have a tendency to plow into large, solid objects like mountains when they leave the wild blue yonder, and then even the dog tags get

An Apache scurries along with its belly in the brush, flying nap-of-the-earth toward a battle position deep in the heart of Texas.

broken. So, from the point of view of Army aviators, the fast movers are relatively useless where it counts, in that big cat fight called the AirLand Battle.

I said before that jet drivers have two problems once their tricycle wheels leave the ground, and the first is finding something useful to do. Well, the other is getting the airplane and themselves back on the ground in one chunk and without any scratches, and again those tiny wings make life difficult. That's why the Navy, Air Force, and Marines all provide their daring young men with a very important piece of equipment — an ejection seat.

The Army's helicopter drivers, however, look at aerial warfare in a completely different way. Instead of pushing the whole airplane through the sky, the helicopter's wings move through the air at flight speed even when the aircraft is still. There are tremendous advantages in a fight. You can see what you are shooting at. You can sneak up on people so they can't see you or shoot at you. You can — thanks to modern technology — even shoot at people you can't see, and be pretty sure of hitting them good and hard. Your base can be any pasture, parking lot, backyard, or hole in the trees big enough for your rotor blades. And Army aviators don't need dotted lines to land or take off. That means they live close to the fight, nearby and neighborly to the folks they're supposed to help.

Helicopters, though, are comparatively difficult to fly, and even Lieutenant Top Gun is likely to make a useless mess of an expensive (and useful) aircraft if he were to try to take off in a helicopter the first time without some expert help.

Admit it — you always wondered what it would be like to fly a helicopter. Here's your chance, and not just any helicopter, either, but the biggest and baddest boy on the block — the AH-64 Apache, nine million dollars worth of black boxes and blades. This is a real honor, because very few people indeed ever get to wedge their rear end into either seat of this airframe. There are only a few hundred Apaches, and much of the information on their displays is classified; but we ought to be able to trust you.

Before we go out to the flight line and sneak off with one, there are some preliminaries that the Army requires. First, you need a flight physical, which will prove that you're warm, not too wide to fit in the seat, and tall enough to see over the instrument panel. Then, you need to be properly attired for the occasion. Starting with basics, you have to wear cotton underwear, since synthetic fabrics melt and stick to the skin in a fire. Over that you wear a Nomex flight suit and gloves, which will protect you against fire for five to ten seconds. The flight suit is comfortable and has pockets that work when you're strapped into your seat. Now you need good Army boots, again for protection when things go bump, and in case we have to walk out from a crash site. Over the flight suit goes the survival vest, containing a small radio, a knife, a signal mirror, and some small items of your choosing. Your head goes into the special helmet used on the Apache, which has a visor you will appreciate in bright sunshine and padding you will appreciate in a crash. There — now you're all dressed up with someplace to go!

You'll find out about the specialized systems of the Apache later; for now we're just going to give you a short course in flying a helicopter. The preflight is complete, so we'll put you in the backseat where the pilot sits. There are steps thought-

Apache pilot and gunner at Fort Hood. *George Hall photo.*

fully placed to help you get up to the little catwalk on the right side. The canopy is already open, so your only problem is to scrunch yourself down and work yourself around the stick until you can sit down. Now, connect the five-point harness and pull the straps tight, and you've got nine million dollars attached to your backside.

Okay, stow any loose gear, adjust the seat and the pedals to suit yourself, and pull the canopy closed and lock it. Put the key in the lock and turn it to the ON position. Normally, we'd go through the full checklist, but just this once we'll keep it to the basics. The engine controls are over on the left; switch ENG 1 and ENG 2 to ON, and make sure the power levers are all the way back at OFF, the engine start switches are OFF, and the master ignition switch is ON. Not much to it! But before

An Apache driver's point of view of the panel, just before taxi. The green screen is a multipurpose display that can be used for navigation, gunnery, and surveillance. Despite a heavy load of computers aboard, the panel is pretty traditional.

things get serious, it's time to pull the pin that safeties the explosive canopy jettison system. Remove it and stow it in its housing, and don't mess with the jettison handle! There's a small cord of explosive that will blast the canopy out of your way on those occasions when you'd rather not see if the Nomex suit and gloves really work.

Now, you'll start the little auxiliary power unit (APU), a small gas turbine that provides electricity and hydraulic power to start up the engines. Flip the BATT switch to ON and you've got elec-

tricity. Press the MASTER CAUTION test switch, and the panel that tells you when you've got problems lights up like a Christmas tree, as it should. The APU panel is hidden over on the right; turn the control switch to RUN, hold it for a moment, then turn it over to START and release it. Sit back and listen to the little turbine as it fires up automatically and its little light illuminates.

Now, make sure the rotor brake is OFF. With the power levers both OFF, turn the ENG START switch to IGN OVRD (which is how aircraft manufacturers spell "ignition override") for thirty seconds, and the start switch to START. You're in business. When the Ng (exhaust gas temperature) peaks at about 25 percent, the power lever goes to IDLE. Monitor the gauges, advance the power lever to FLY, and then do the same with the other engine. Gosh! That's all there is to it, and you can take to the skies.

Once you push the throttles of the Apache forward into FLY, the helicopter is ready to go to work. One of the many black boxes aboard will control the amount of fuel sent to the engines based on your control input, so the application of power is automatic. A helicopter driver has two primary controls, both attached to the long wings revolving overhead. Your left hand grasps a large

An AH-64 Apache comes to a hover at Fort Rucker before going off to practice low-level flight above the rolling terrain of southern Alabama. The Apache, with its great weight and stability augmentation system, hovers easily.

The gunner in the front seat looks for targets while the pilot of Gremlin 30 slides the helicopter around a small hill in Fort Hood's tactical training area. The intelligent use of terrain masking is a fundamental part of Army tactics.

lever called the COLLECTIVE, for collective pitch control. By raising this control, you adjust the pitch in all four of the blades at once, like pulling up the nose in a fixed-wing aircraft. The computer adds fuel to the engine to maintain power, and the blades all start producing lift. First, the helicopter feels light on the gear; then as the wheels start to clear the ground, the helicopter will want to spin on its axis—a result of the torque applied to the rotor. You counteract this with opposite pedal—not too much, just enough! Everybody tries to use too much control input the first time. The big trick with helicopters, as in life, is to correct your mistakes and don't overcorrect! Your mistakes will become progressively smaller, and after a bit you will slip the surly bonds of earth.

Now that we're off the ground and not spinning like a top, we are balanced in a hover on a slippery pile of compressed air, and it is very difficult to keep from sliding off. The stick between your knees is called the CYCLIC, for cyclic pitch control, and it has the effect of tilting the whole plane of rotating blades above you. Push it forward and the spinning set of blades tilts forward. At a hover like this, it takes tiny little inputs to stay in one spot, but beginners always try great big inputs, with the result that they go squirting all over the landscape. It doesn't take long to learn to hover, but it is a different kind of takeoff than a jet driver uses; you are busy with both hands and both feet. The first few times feel like the first time you tried to ride a bicycle, times ten.

After getting control of the helicopter in a hover to the extent that you can keep it in one or two counties, it's time to take off. This is easier than hovering; just push forward on the cyclic and the helicopter will tilt and start to move forward. Pull up gradually on the collective and you will climb up and away; and if you don't use the pedals to counteract the changing amounts of torque going to the rotor blades, you'll find yourself moving in directions you hadn't intended. As the aircraft picks up speed it becomes more and more stable and easy to control, and by the time the airspeed indicator is pointing at thirty knots or so, it is about as easy to control as any magic carpet.

By careful use of the collective and cyclic controls, you can glide across the treetops in a way far more delightful than any jet driver ever experiences at altitude. One hundred knots of airspeed just above the contours of the ground gives a sensation of tremendous speed, power, and control. You can make the helicopter flow along the ups and downs of the terrain like a bird—a wonderful experience that permits flight down twisting little creeks, up small ravines, across and in between trees. The Army calls this "nap–of–the–earth" (NOE) flight, and not only is it fun, it is tactically useful, although somewhat dangerous because of wires. Pull gently back on the cyclic and lower the collective, add pedal to keep from spinning, and you can come to a hover with the aircraft inches above the trees to inspect some object on the ground. Since you're in an Apache and have the resources of the integrated helmet and display sight system (IHADS) and the helmet mounted display (HMD), you can look outside the cockpit in any direction and still see a full set of navigation, weapons, and engine information.

Push forward on the cyclic, add collective, correct torque with the pedals, and off we go again with a limitless sense of power and control. Compared to earlier helicopters, the Apache is very stable and easy to control. Part of this comes from the automation that takes a lot of the work load away from the pilot and gives it to black boxes throughout the aircraft. Most Army helicopters are now equipped with stability augmentation systems, which reduce the amount of work required to control the aircraft. They really perform quite well. You can take your hands off cyclic and collective at a hover and you will continue to hover; previously this was a great way to ruin a perfectly good aircraft. The Apache even has a hover-hold switch, which will make things easier in those tactical situations where you need to do ten things at once.

Well, it's almost time to get this thing back to the barn, so let's pull pitch. Add a lot of forward cyclic and a lot of collective, and you will find the dial in the middle of the panel indicating 140 knots, about 160 miles an hour . . . and here we

Apache taxis out for take off. *George Hall photo.*

are, right back at that cozy nook we call home. Aft cyclic, lower the collective, maintain heading with the pedals, and we slow down and settle down to a hover about ten feet above the ground. Carefully hover-taxi back to the little spot we left, lower the collective gradually, and feel for the ground until the gear touches. There is a shutdown checklist to follow in order to be kind to the engines and other systems, including a cool down for the turbines. All of the switches must be returned to their proper positions; then at last you shut down the engines, stop the rotors with the rotor brakes, and turn off all the systems in the checklist sequence. You become aware of how quiet it is and how sweaty your palms are. There, we've cheated death again!

A Concise History of the Army and Airplanes

If you paid much attention to the Air Force and the Navy, you'd think they invented the airplane and the best way to use it. The U.S. Army doesn't get much credit in discussions about the evolution of aviation or even of military aviation. The glory goes to the big bombers and the jet fighters of the Air Force or Navy, but it should be going to the Army, because it has been right out in front since before the Wright brothers were in knee pants.

The Army actually started using aviation back in the early 1860s, during the Civil War, with balloons to lift artillery observers high above the ground, so they could see where the cannon shots were falling. The corrections they provided the gunners made for more effective and economical shooting. And the observers were pleased to discover that although they were certainly visible to the enemy, they were just about impossible to shoot down. During a battle in May 1862, quick action and accurate observation by Thaddeus Lowe, transmitted by telegraph from high above the fight, was instrumental in preventing a defeat by Confederate forces.

About four decades later, after years of experiments and failures, the first powered aircraft took to the skies from Kitty Hawk, North Carolina. It took the Wright brothers very little time to decide who ought to be interested in their invention, and they offered the U.S. Army the first crack at the chance to buy some. The Army, in its traditional way, refused to admit that powered flight was possible—for three years after the Wrights demonstrated that it could be done. They made hundreds of flights in the vicinity of Dayton, Ohio, and then in Europe before convincing the Army that powered flight was indeed possible. The Army then scheduled tests at Fort McNair. In 1908, during one of these tests, a young officer named Lt. Thomas Selfridge, flying as a passenger, became aviation's first fatality when the plane crashed. The casualty dampened the Army's interest a bit, and the Wrights ended up selling their patents.

When World War I began eleven years after the Wright brothers' first flight, aviation had developed to a tremendous degree, and military aviation was (then as now) the leading edge. The U.S. Army became the custodian for aviation primarily because it was thought that the airplane would be useful for artillery spotting. The Europeans found other things to do with airplanes and started mounting guns and bomb racks on them. It took very little time before all the basic missions of air forces today were being accomplished, including air to air, recon, air to ground, bombing, transport, and so forth. Although American aviators didn't fly American combat aircraft but used British and French models instead, they came away with an evangelist's enthusiasm for this new technology.

After the "war to end all wars," the American defense establishment was reduced to nearly nothing; all that was left of our air forces were a few bombers and fighters, and a lot of frustration on the part of those aviators who remained in the tiny Army of the 1920s. Defense policy once again stressed naval power as the first priority of the armed forces, based on the impressive bulk, speed, and firepower of the battleship. These huge vessels were stoutly armored, and govern-

Igor Sikorsky at the controls of one of his early designs. Loud, weak, and windy, it still got off the ground, demonstrating the helicopter's potential. Flight suits no longer feature overcoats or homburg crash helmets. *Sikorsky Aircraft*.

ment policy makers, in and out of the military, considered them unsinkable by air attack. A lot of aviators thought otherwise, but only a few were in a position to say so with authority.

One of these was Col. Billy Mitchell, whose vision of military aviation was not shared by many of his superiors. Mitchell had a sense of audacity, imagination, and urgency that is shared by soldiers who excel in wartime. These sort of men tend to play the political games of peacetime rather badly, and so it was with Mitchell. (Mitchell had actually planned the first paratroop operation in history, had gotten a favorable response from Gen. John Pershing, and would have executed it in the spring of 1919 if the war had continued.) Mitchell saw that air power had changed the rules of the game, and that as the technology of aviation advanced, the United States population centers and military forces could be quickly attacked from far over the horizon. He contended that the huge, powerful warships that had always been the pride and foundation of our forces had suddenly become vulnerable to small, comparatively inexpensive weapons.

Mitchell bent regulations in his crusade to demonstrate that his airplanes could defeat major surface ships. To the dismay of many in the naval community, in 1921, only eighteen years after Kitty Hawk, Mitchell was able to put on a demonstration off the Virginia Capes of what airplanes could do. Using Martin MB-2 bombers dropping 2,000-pound bombs, Mitchell's force sent a battleship to the bottom in only twenty-two minutes while many of the observing naval officers fought back tears.

This demonstration proved Mitchell's contention—and proved to be his downfall when he used it to loudly demand a separate Air Service with

An early Wright design being prepared for Army trials at Fort McNair. Lt. Thomas Selfridge died in this aircraft later in the day, earning the honor of becoming the first heavier-than-air craft fatality. *National Air & Space Museum/Arms Communications.*

modern equipment and missions. Mitchell had been right in the wrong way; he was court-martialed in 1926 for "insubordination and conduct unbecoming of an officer." He was convicted and reduced in rank, resigned from the Air Service, and relegated to an obscure position. He died without seeing his vision and his warning fulfilled on 7 December 1941.

Although Mitchell was denounced, his arguments were largely accepted, and in fact the Air Service became the Air Corps about the time Mitchell was convicted. And the War Department acquired an assistant secretary for air, a signal that the message was received even if the messenger had bad breath.

During the years between the world wars, military aviation developed at a spectacular pace, with the Army out front in many areas. The technologies of the time produced faster, more complex designs and systems, with new fighting doctrine to match. Quick, little pursuit planes and big bombers with five-man crews came off the drawing boards and off to squadrons around the world. The depression cut into funding, but it didn't cut into the imaginations of American planners, or those of the Germans and Japanese.

The Germans flew the first real helicopter in 1936, but Igor Sikorsky wasn't far behind in the U.S. He flew the VS-300 in 1939 and in 1940 got a contract from the Army. During World War II, a few R-4B helicopters actually served with Army combat units.

Military aviation quickly developed into a huge and essential component of the strategic forces of the country. The American public as well as the entire military watched in awe as the Germans used air power to force their political vision on unwilling countries; first Spain, then Poland and the Low Countries, then France fell through a combination of air, armor, artillery, and infantry attack. The Battle of Britain was a lesson in the new political reality. The English survived because of three fortunate resources: the Channel; a "hard-core" attitude; and a plan of battle that integrated radar, ground/air coordination, and excellent Hurricane and Spitfire aircraft.

Although some lessons were learned, the U.S. military received a failing grade when the Japanese dropped in at Pearl Harbor in December 1941 and found the Navy aircraft and ships lined up nice and neat. Although much has been said about the loss of the Pacific Fleet in that attack, the bulk of American air power in the Pacific was also lost at Pearl and the other bases that were attacked in the next few weeks. Until the attack, many in the United States believed that Americans could isolate themselves from the conflict, and resisted military preparedness in any form. Afterward, these same people wanted blood.

The Army and Navy both integrated aviation into their individual schemes of battle. Air power in World War II was used for a tremendous variety of strategic and tactical purposes. The big, strategic uses involved bombing enemy population and manufacturing centers in an effort to attack the basic economies of the Axis powers, a campaign of tremendous cost in people and machines, and with somewhat dubious results. (The Germans continued to crank out all sorts of war materiel long after their cities were smoking piles of rubble.) There were also frequent uses of aviation in direct tactical support of battles and campaigns on the ground. Although the helicopter was not a practical technology at this time, the feasibility of airmobility and air assault operations was clearly demonstrated by the Germans in the early years of the war. Their brilliant paratroop operations in Poland and Belgium and on Crete amazed Allied planners, who hurriedly developed similar programs.

In the United States, testing of parachute operations did not even begin until 1940, only four years before two entire divisions would be dropped into France on the night of 5–6 June 1944. And while the strategic and tactical missions were getting headlines and glory, literally thousands of Army aerial trucks in the form of the C-47 twin-engined cargo planes carried food, fuel, medicine, replacements, equipment, USO tours, ammunition, mail, vehicles, artillery pieces, and almost anything else that would fit through the doors or attach to the wings of the glorious "gooney bird."

Igor Sikorsky and the Coast Guard's R-4B in 1944. Similar versions were used by the Army, but both had problems with limited power and control, and were not terribly useful. Note that Igor has disposed of the homburg and overcoat; can brain buckets and flight suits be far behind? *Sikorsky Aircraft.*

Although millions of sorties were flown, only three basic kinds of missions were performed, and these three remain the foundation for Army aviation today. The first, *combat*, involved the intentional and direct engagement of the enemy, either on the ground or in the air. The fighters and bombers of this era were combat aircraft. The second mission, *combat support*, involved helping somebody else fight, as the C-47s did when they carried the 82d and 101st Airborne Divisions into battle. The third mission, *combat service support*, involved helping sustain the fight with resupply of beans and bullets. In theory, any aircraft can fly any of these missions, but in fact most are designed for one or the other.

By the end of World War II, the Air Corps had become such a large and loud institution, with objectives that seemed far more strategic than tactical, that it was removed from the Army, and the Air Force was born. At the time there was tremendous concern in the Army that the new organization would lose sight of its tactical (as opposed to strategic) missions and wouldn't be around when some battalion of infantry was nose to nose with a horde of bad guys and needed help. And that's exactly what happened. The development of the atomic bomb changed the way a lot of people thought about warfare, and a fair number of Pentagon planners concluded that the common foot soldier was about to be a footnote in the history of conflict. The kinds of aircraft being designed and purchased for the new Air Force were big bombers designed to carry atomic weapons deep into the Soviet Union, and were of little use in support of the infantry.

One group of military planners, however, had full faith in the ability of infantry to achieve strategic victories, and this group was the government of North Korea. When they attacked across the border in 1950, it was against a flimsy defense by units of the South Korean armed forces. There were few resources available to stop these massive attacks by hundreds of thousands of infantry, except atomic weapons, and they had been rendered ineffective by political decisions. South Korea's survival was bought with infantry blood, in huge quantities. It took awhile for the United Nations to react effectively, and in the end the invasion was pushed back, through the combined efforts of land, sea, and air forces of several nations.

The terrain of Korea is steep, often muddy, and impassable for wheeled vehicles. So the effortless and rapid flights of the new H-13 helicopter in support of the infantry made a powerful first impression. These little helicopters were just about the only aviation assets the Army was allowed to retain when the Air Force split away with the big systems. By comparison to the aircraft of the time, the H-13 was almost a toy, with its one pilot and either a couple of hundred

pounds of cargo or one or two passengers. But in Korea in 1952, the cargo was often ammunition or food for units that couldn't get resupplied any other way, and the passengers were wounded, being miraculously transported to medics and hospitals in minutes instead of days.

These helicopters made such an impression that commanders started experimenting with them for all kinds of missions, even mounting machine guns on them and trying them for direct support of infantry. Now, this mission of close air support was supposed to be performed by the Air Force, Navy, and Marines, who were often good about trying to accomplish it; but several factors conspired against them. One was their fighter aircraft, which were not designed for ground attack but for air-to-air missions; they flew too fast to accurately deliver the weapons they carried. Another factor was the terrain of Korea itself, its steep hills providing defenders cover and concealment against low-flying, high-performance aircraft. And yet another was the skill of the North Koreans in exploiting the weaknesses of the aircraft of the time: they simply hid during the day and moved at night to avoid attack by high-altitude bombers.

So the commanders looked with lust and longing at the few little helicopters that had come to call. And they got what they wanted; from a total of about 700 aircraft in the inventory in 1950, Army aviation grew to more than 5,000 aircraft in fifteen varieties by 1960—helicopters and fixed-wing aircraft, big and small, for all sorts of missions. Army aviation had become a big issue, with bigger visions for the future.

But the Air Force didn't like it. A dispute developed about who owned what part of the sky, and both sides won on some points. The Air

Force defended its turf, and the Army lost some of its aircraft and missions. But the fundamental decision was made, allowing the Army to develop a kind of "sky cavalry," and a whole new family of aircraft began to be imagined, designed, built, fielded, and flown. The age of military helicopters truly began.

Development of the helicopter progressed during the Korean War. The problems were several: it was an inherently unstable machine, and consequently difficult to fly; it was inefficient, needing lots of power to lift a small payload; and it was complicated. The air-cooled internal combustion technology of the 1950s produced relatively little power at the cost of a lot of weight, and the helicopters of the time were rather wimpy. Even helo drivers said (and still say, for that matter) that helicopters don't really fly, they just beat the air into submission. Nevertheless, under pressure from the Army, helicopters were designed that could actually lift a whole squad of soldiers and carry them into battle. These aircraft were underpowered and unstable, but they worked. The H-19, H-34, and H-21 designs of the late 1950s (when they worked) were able to carry entire infantry companies and even battalions into battle, and the Marines as well as the Army began experimenting with airmobility. Both learned a lot and (since it was wartime) actually shared with each other.

The technology changed dramatically when the gas turbine engine became a practical reality for designers in the mid 1950s, and they started building airframes around the idea. The gas turbine is, in many ways, the foundation of Army aviation today. Because of this engine's light weight, small volume, high power, and great reliability, helicopters have become a major ele-ment of and a sustainer behind combat power on the battlefield.

The first really successful design based on the turbine was the UH-1; the Army nicknamed it the "Iroquois," but the troops have always called it "Huey," "Slick," or "Slug." When the Huey started to be deployed in 1962, it transformed the way commanders thought about aviation. The aircraft was so successful that it continues to serve today, almost thirty years after it was designed.

At about this time the United States began sending soldiers to an obscure Southeast Asian nation to advise and support a friendly but beleaguered third-world country. Viet Nam was still struggling, a decade and a half after the end of World War II, with the residue of global politics and the demise of colonialism. President John Kennedy was commander in chief, and he had some radical ideas about the role of the United States in the world and the responsibilities and missions of the armed forces to support that role. The result was a shift away from a focus on nuclear conflict and global war toward smaller, more primitive encounters. Viet Nam provided a chance for a comparatively inexpensive test of Kennedy's ideas in a real world situation. So starting in 1960, American "advisers" started taking to the field all over South Viet Nam; beginning in 1961 they included helicopters and crews.

The first contingent arrived in December 1961 — thirty-two H-21 Shawnee helicopters from the 57th Helicopter Company at Fort Lewis and the 8th Transportation Company (Light Helicopter) from Fort Bragg. Four-hundred pilots and crew and support people got off the little aircraft carrier USNS *Card* in Saigon, joining other American military personnel dispersed around the country. Only twelve days later the two companies

Not the first bullet hole, and certainly not the last, it was still too close for comfort when a bullet missed this gunner by about a foot in 1963 in the highlands of Viet Nam. It was discovered that helicopters could absorb a lot of such holes before something (or someone) important got hit.

were used in combat in Operation Chopper: a thousand ARVN Rangers were lifted into a VC headquarters complex near the capital. The operation surprised the enemy, who were accustomed to having plenty of warning when government troops started blundering across the countryside in their direction. The VC were surprised, but not so much so that they neglected to fire at the helicopters. The helicopters didn't shoot back, though; they were completely without weapons.

This mission on 23 December 1961 marks the first trial by fire of American helicopter systems and tactics, a theory of airmobility that had been evolving since the Test Platoon at Fort Benning had experimented with parachutes at the beginning of World War II.

Over the next few months in Viet Nam, Army aviation began to develop rapidly; the units were no longer training for war but participating in one. The 8th Trans shipped out to the little coastal city of Qui Nhon, where it began flying missions throughout the central part of the country with its banana-shaped aircraft. It was joined by other helicopter companies at Pleiku and elsewhere. It didn't take long for the VC to start putting holes in the sheet metal of the helicopters and earning the resentment of the aircrews and their commanders. This resentment was intensified when holes started appearing in the crewmen themselves, and shortly thereafter permission was granted to put weapons on the helicopters.

These H-21s had two doors, and each had a .30-caliber M1919-A6 air-cooled machine gun on an improvised mount manufactured by the hangar crews. There were problems that took some time to overcome: the latch that held the gun to the mount would occasionally come undone, and the weapon would fall out of the sky, trailing a belt of ammunition. The Army gets very upset about the loss of weapons, and the poor gunners would watch in horror as their weapons fell away through space. But the guns worked fairly well, if only to give the crews a feeling that they could give as well as take.

The helicopter crews quickly learned to improvise. One of the best places to do this was on the frequent flights into the jungle, where the Special Forces (Green Berets to most people) teams had set up shop. At the time, vast quantities of old weapons were being dispensed to the villagers, and nobody was bothering with petty details like record keeping. So the crews "bor-rowed" extra backup weapons, and it wasn't long before the helicopters had stashes of personal machine guns, grenades, and pistols.

There were times when the crews were glad to have these weapons, because the H-21 was hardly equal to its task and frequently crashed. The survivors sometimes had to fight off the bad guys before being rescued.

It wasn't long before the helicopter units started taking casualties, and—although the news media wasn't paying much attention—the numbers of people were significant. But the planners at the Pentagon and at Fort Rucker's Army Aviation Center were paying close attention. Although the H-21 was obviously a wimpy machine, the planners knew that better helicopters would be available soon, with far more power and capability. The question was not "can helicopters carry soldiers into battle?" but rather "can aviation make a significant difference on the battlefield?" And the answer they were getting from Viet Nam was: maybe.

It was clear that Army aviation was performing its missions: delivering troops into battle, retrieving the dead and wounded from remote locations, providing supplies and people to outposts that would otherwise be untenable. But what wasn't clear was the ability of aviation to coordinate with a battlefield scheme of maneuver, the ability to make a difference in major battles and campaigns. A definitive conclusion was complicated by the fact that the ARVN soldiers were very spotty in their performance. In theory, the ARVN should have been able to eat up the VC, with their primitive weapons and small numbers. But the ARVN commanders had other battles to fight—political battles—and the ones out in the jungle tended to take a lower priority. With an aggressive commander and good soldiers, the helicopters often made a significant difference. But for many reasons the helicopters were employed as a kind of small sideshow rather than as a foundation for a major effort on the battlefield, and without real coordination with other elements.

The man in charge of making the big decisions at the time was Secretary of Defense Robert McNamara, and he was concerned about the nature and direction of Army aviation. He prodded the Army to reexamine its requirements in light of new technologies becoming available and the changing vision of conflict by the new administration. The result was the Howze Board, whose mandate was to look long, hard, and imaginatively at the future Army and the future of aviation in it. Out of the board's study came the concept of an "air assault" division, a synthesis of infantry and its supporting units with aviation in a truly integrated force.

The vision was of an infantry division to which was grafted a huge aviation component of nearly 500 aircraft. The aircraft were not just to support the infantry, but to be a part of it, very much like the age-old concept of cavalry. This division, as imagined, would do away with most of the wheeled vehicles of a normal infantry unit and much of the heavy artillery as well. Its organic aircraft could move a third of a division in one go. It would include something called an "air cavalry combat brigade," with 316 aircraft, half of which were to be attack helicopters—at a time when most of the Army wouldn't recognize an attack helicopter if it bit them on the foot. The whole concept would provide a commander with combat power and a new potential for exploiting the principles of what is now called AirLand Battle: initiative, agility, depth, and synchronization.

But the idea was just that—an idea—and only parts of it could be tested in Viet Nam. The board suggested a formal examination of the concept, and in February 1963 the colors of the 11th Airborne Division of World War II were reactivated as the 11th Air Assault Division at Fort Benning, Georgia.

The 11th started acquiring some of the new aircraft the Army had ordered back in the 1950s, including lots of Hueys and Chinooks, a few gigantic CH-54s, plus all sorts of other designs. There were still a few piston-powered dinosaurs on the ramp at Lawson Field, but they were soon replaced by a younger generation of machines with more power, speed, and reliability than the crews or commanders had ever seen.

The 11th was supposed to be an experiment, so during the training and equipping phase a kind of yeasty atmosphere existed in which all sorts of ideas were tried and evaluated. Thousands of the best aviators and infantry struggled together with new aircraft and new ideas about how to use them. Rules about where you could fly and how you could fly were relaxed, and pilots found themselves blasting along under low overcasts, tucked into tight formations, and flying missions previously prohibited.

Then, in October and November 1964, the whole concept was tested by 35,000 players and evaluators in a huge scenario called Air Assault II. It involved the 11th Air Assault Division fighting the 82d Airborne "bad guys" all over the Carolinas. And it was a success: the concept of an airmobile organization the size of a division was validated with enthusiasm. It was opportune, because the situation in Viet Nam was turning into what soldiers call a "goatscrew," a disorganized and inefficient chaos unlikely to achieve

the desired result. Americans would be going to Southeast Asia in large numbers just to keep Viet Nam from collapsing.

In March 1965, the decision was made to convert the 11th to an official member of the force structure, but with some changes in the grand Army tradition. The new division would assume the colors and lineage of the dear old 1st Cavalry, then serving in Korea. It would be made from the 11th Air Assault (Test) and the 2d Infantry Division, and its official name would be the 1st

A squad of infantry "unass the bird" from about six feet above South Viet Nam. This exit technique was safer for the helicopter and allowed troops to be delivered to places previously inaccessible. Until the Huey and its gas turbine engine came along, such exploits were impossible. *Bell Helicopter Textron*.

Cavalry Division (Airmobile). The ink was hardly dry in the signature blocks of General Order 185 before the new division was on its way to Viet Nam.

The 1st Air Cav (as it was popularly called) set up shop just up the road from Qui Nhon back in the mountains near a little village called An Khe. Out of the jungle was built a raw foundation for the 16,000 soldiers of the division who soon arrived and declared hunting season open, with no bag limits and no safe areas.

At about this time the NVA began an operation intended to cut the country in half, beginning with an attack on a Special Forces (SF) camp at Plei Me not far from An Khe. The result was an education for both sides in airmobility.

Just a year after Air Assault II had validated the idea that helicopters could change some of the fundamental techniques of combat, another large-scale test was ordered. This time it was against the NVA's 32d, 33d, and 66th regiments in the battle of the Ia Drang Valley. It began on 1 November when an intelligence officer spotted what turned out to be an enemy hospital just eight klicks from the SF camp and sent out the Air Cav squadron's rifle and gunship platoons to investigate. In the fight that followed, seventy-eight NVA were killed and fifty-seven captured; five Americans were killed and seventeen wounded. It was the opening act in what would be a long play.

During the twelve years or so of American Army aviation involvement in Viet Nam, many units besides the 1st Air Cav fought and supported allied units. The evolution of both technology and tactics during this time was frantic, and much of the current systems and doctrine have their roots in the events of the 1960s and early 1970s. Skirmishes were fought with other services as well as with the NVA and VC, and the Army lost some of its aircraft to the Air Force in a turf dispute in 1966. But the history of Army aviation was and is written by the experience of individuals who use the systems and execute the doctrine day to day. Here's what one pilot, still serving,

still in "guns," remembers about this time:

The kinds of missions that I flew as an assault helicopter gunship driver were primarily combat assault, and it was our job to cover the lift helicopters going in and out of the LZ. This was different from a Cav unit, whose basic mission was to go out, find, seek, and destroy. This was before the era of missiles, so safety was at altitude, so if you were above 2,000 feet, you were safe because small arms became ineffective, and the closer you got to the ground, the more dangerous it got. The most vulnerable time was going into and out of the LZ and especially on the ground, so that required a lot of LZ prep. If we expected bad guys to be there, we would prep the LZ with rockets and machine guns. A lot of times, it would appear to only be trees and an open field; we'd put "nails," rockets, and minigun rounds down through the trees, see nothing, receive no fire, call the "slicks" on in, and when the guys get in the trees they say there are dead people everywhere! So it was not uncommon at all to have engagements and have kills where you never saw anything at all.

We had five Charlie models [Hueys] in a platoon, with a heavy team of three and a light team of two. A light team would usually have one helicopter in a minigun configuration and the other would be in heavy rocket configuration, and door gunners on both sides with M-60 machine guns on bungee cords. The door gunners were just for self protection.

Any more than three gunships on an operation was rare, and the only time that was likely to happen was for a "tac E," or tactical emergency, meaning some ground unit had gotten into some situation where they needed close air support immediately. Even then we would rotate light and heavy sections, one on station and the other off getting fuel and ammunition, then swap so we could maintain some kind of continuous pressure. We used all kinds of patterns: "racetrack," "clover-leaf," and so forth, the intention of which was to keep continuous fire on the target.

It was generally quite effective—for the time, before the era of missiles. The name of the game then was to get the firepower on them while you are out of their effective range, and as you come into their effective range, break it. Sometimes you couldn't avoid it, especially if the slicks got into trouble in the LZ, you had to get in there with them, go face-to-face.

I got shot down three times, but always as a slick driver, before I got in guns, inserting troops into hot LZs and just got unlucky.

The engine was instantly gone with a loud KABOOM and we were low and slow, maybe fifty feet over the trees just short of the LZ and there were no options; it was right here, right now, so we autorotated into the trees. Once you contact the trees with the blades, you are no longer in control, you are basically a passenger in a tumbling object. The trees were small, so we all got out without any major injuries, but there was a firefight maybe fifty meters from us, with the bad guys between us and the LZ and bullets going through the trees overhead. It took about an hour for them to provide enough suppression to let us get to the LZ and for them to come in and get us. It was tense.

The Army put its helicopters and crews through a wringer, and it was costly. By 1971, 4,200 helicopters had been lost. While most were due to mechanical failure, still 45 percent was the result of hostile fire. The helicopters of the time were extremely vulnerable under the conditions in which they fought. Just the same, they were pushed hard: many helicopters had flown 18,000 combat sorties before being lost.

The battle experience of Viet Nam changed forever the way the Army thought about aviation, and the concept of airmobility was incorporated into the force structure in a way many found highly traumatic. For several decades, airmobility had meant parachutes, and was the exclusive province of the proud airborne divisions whose members have never been considered shy or reserved about their exalted status as the hardest of the hard core. They have referred to nonairborne units as "leg" outfits, a disparaging comment on the cowardly way most infantry is transported to battle.

The 101st was one of five airborne divisions during World War II, back when airmobility depended on parachutes, which were the only way to quickly deliver people, equipment, and supplies into battle. It was, forty years ago, an acceptable way to do business, and it got the job done in Normandy, Sicily, Corregidor, and elsewhere, but at a high cost. Losses for the jump into Normandy were expected to be 50 percent and the operation was mounted anyway. After the war, three of the five divisions were eliminated, their colors retired, leaving only the 82d and 101st on duty until October of 1973, when the lessons of the 11th Air Assault, then the 1st Air Cav, indicated a need for a change.

That change came for the 101st at Fort Campbell, Kentucky, with a change of mission: instead of airborne, the division became airmobile, to the long, loud protests of a multitude of professional parachutists. To no avail. The change was permanent, so the troopers decided to make the air assault badge as difficult to get as the paratrooper's wings had always been. They set up a course, and gradually pushed the entire division through it, training everybody in the new doctrine. Now air assault courses are available on most installations, and the skills required for airmobile tactics are taught to people in many kinds of units.

The history of Army aviation is also the history of the evolution of weapons systems and aircraft. It's interesting how much of contemporary weapons and tactics have their origins in Southeast Asia twenty years ago; even the glorious Apache was a twinkle in the eye of some designer shortly after the 1st Air Cav went to work in Viet Nam.

Today's Cobra, the E model, is the great grandchild of the late, great AH-1 that deployed to Viet Nam in 1967. That ancestor was the first dedicated gunship and replaced earlier helicopters like the OH-6A and UH-1, which had been modified by the addition of guns and rockets. And it was a good thing, too. If you've ever seen a Huey head-on, as numerous VC certainly have, you know what you want in a target: a big, fat, slow aircraft, with its pilots sitting right there in the window like targets in a shooting gallery. If it were not for some pretty bold tactics, a lot more of the guns would have thrashed out of the sky in "baby grand" mode.

During those endless moments when the gunships were laying flame and fury on the forces of evil, and dodging the great balls of green fire coming right back, their pilots thought a lot about what they'd really like to have in a gunship design. Something with the smallest possible profile, for starters. Then, something with lots of firepower—none of this paltry 7.62mm stuff. Lots of rockets, and a way to lay them on hot and heavy. A cannon, with its explosive projectiles, would be swell, too. Then, if you please, how about a grenade launcher that would spit out 40mm high-explosive warheads. Give us some armor, some speed, and put it all together in the skinniest little target in the air.

The A model was a start, and it arrived in 1967, not much more than a radically customized UH-1 with one of the pilots now sitting in back. The pilots really liked its narrow profile, about one fourth the width of the Huey; the back seater in particular liked it, because it put the gunner between him and any bullets coming up from the target. It carried a lot of stuff—too much for its little engine; if you could get it off the ground, however, it would put some serious hurt on the enemy. But in order to get into the high, hot, humid air of Asia with a full load of weapons, something had to be left off. Normally this was fuel. So the A models would jam on out to the party, make a pass or two at one of the guests, and run home again. It is the nature of an A model that there are things to be improved, and they were. Over the months and years, the Cobra became an essential player in the Army aviation game.

It inspired work on an even more capable helicopter. Even before the Cobra shipped out for the war zone, the Army had let a contract for the advanced attack helicopter (AAH), the granddaddy of the Apache. The result of this contract was an extraordinary design called the AH-56 Cheyenne, a marvel that flew for the first time in 1967. The Cheyenne was powered by a 3,435-horsepower engine, driving a four-bladed rotor system. It was good for 220 knots, but that was not good enough. While the designers were busy solving the problems of the attack mission in

Asia, the NVA, VC, and Soviets were busy changing the rules. The SA-7 heat-seeking missile began zipping up to greet helicopters flying at treetop elevations, and the high speed of the AH-56 was no longer such a hot priority. What was needed was a helicopter that could essentially hover-taxi into battle, staying down below the treetops, using cover and concealment for protection the way an infantryman does. What was also needed was protection for the crew when (as happened frequently) cover and concealment weren't enough and little chunks of metal went zooming through U.S. government property and personnel.

The specs were rewritten and the Cheyenne couldn't meet them. What the Army asked for in 1972 was an aircraft that would be happy flying and fighting NOE (nap of the earth) day; night; in bad weather; in a front-line battlefield; in a low-, medium-, or high-intensity threat environment. It didn't need to do 220 knots—145 would be okay. But it had to carry eight TOW missiles and fly combat sorties almost two hours long. Its performance specs were not for the traditional sea level but for 4,000 feet on a 95-degree day—the kind of conditions found in Viet Nam. The emphasis was shifted to maneuverability and the ability to jerk around the helicopter at high g loadings without having the blades break or things fall off. Then, the Army asked for the ability to take .50-caliber hits and an occasional 23mm cannon shell without coming apart at the seams. On top of it all, the Army wanted an airframe that could come thrashing out of the sky at forty-two feet per second (thirty miles per hour), slam to the ground, and still give the crew a 95 percent chance to survive. That was a tall order for a helicopter.

The specs were changed from TOWs to Hellfire missiles as the latter began to take life on the drawing board, and that change meant a lot of extra weight. The Cobra, all fat and happy, weighed about 6,500 pounds as it left for work; the new AAH was starting to look like about 13,000 pounds. To haul all that stuff into the sky meant two engines, one of which should act as a spare in case it was needed. Although the Army didn't actually require it, the GE YT-700 then in development for the UH-60 was a natural choice.

The Cobra had shown that a chin-mounted cannon in a flexible turret was a great lifesaver. The M197 20mm cannon also had been a big hit, but the new helicopter needed something with more range and power. Multibarreled Gatling guns had been working well on the Air Force's fighters, and were considered. But the Hughes chain gun design beat them out, and another part of the design was cast into concrete.

The systems used today are really evolutions of requirements identified twenty years ago, refined and developed as new technologies and new opportunities come along. Some of these have been tested in combat, in the brief firefights that the Army has been involved in, both in Grenada and in the little pirate skirmishes in the Persian Gulf.

The history of Army aviation (like the history of anything) can be fascinating, because by looking back you can also look forward. What it tells us is the Army has always been willing to consider new technologies from the moment they become possible, and sometimes well before. The Army's use of aerial observers during the Civil War demonstrated the kind of audacity that is alive and well in all sorts of programs and systems in the field and in development today. The Army is a rich mixture of the highest and the lowest kinds of technologies, of ancient traditions and brand new procedures.

Guns!
The Apache and Cobra

There are at least two good ways to settle a dispute. If you're big and bad enough, you can find the offending party and just pile on until one of you quits. If the offending party is bigger and badder, you can sneak up on him, get in a few licks, and run like crazy. If you keep this up long enough, you can wear down your stronger opponent and use up his strength. The aviation assets of the Army are designed to do both, and both are the missions of the Army's two attack helicopters, the Apache and the Cobra.

The attack helicopters have two major missions. The first is the *combat* or *attack* role. Such missions can involve strikes against enemy armor, troops, artillery, installations, or anything else that is part of the fight. The second major mission is called *cavalry*, and involves indirect attacks against the enemy. Both of these missions are done by the Cobra and the Apache. As one aviation battalion commander says, "If you don't know exactly where the enemy is or what he's doing, then the smart thing to do is to send in the spies, and that's the mission of the Air Cavalry. Once you find him, then you can send in a hit team to beat him up, and that's the attack mission."

The Army's got two helicopters that are designed for the attack and cav missions, the attack helicopters AH-1 (the Cobra) and AH-64 (the Apache). Both can perform either mission, but the Cobra was designed for low- and mid-intensity attack missions and is more of a day fighter than the Apache. Neither aircraft will normally get sent out by itself to perform either mis-

sion. Teams are assembled for specific missions, a process called "task organization." There are scout/weapons teams, where an observation helicopter goes looking for trouble, escorted by one or two Cobras or Apaches; there are also "hunter-killer" teams, "pink" teams, and "heavy-light" teams, each with its own set of virtues and vices.

COBRA

The Cobra was designed to be the first dedicated helicopter gunship, an evolution of the early UH-1 experiments. During Viet Nam the Cobra earned its spurs as the faithful air cover that the "grunts" could depend on when the Air Force jets couldn't (or wouldn't) get under the clouds. The "snakes" could cut loose rockets, machine gun fire, and 40mm grenades, although they suffered in the process, with their single engine, minimal armor, and dangerous mission. But the basic airframe and basic mission proved too valuable to discard, so the Cobra has grown up alongside the Chinook as Army aviation evolved.

Despite the glory that goes to the Apache these days, one of the most challenging, difficult, and important missions in the Air Cav book of tricks might be the "scout-weapons" role performed by two helicopters working together as a team. Although the Apache can perform the scout role well, it is often the Cobra that is tasked with the job. Teamed with the marvelous OH-58 Kiowa, the Cobra is a potent resource for any commander. These two rather elderly airframes have been tricked out with the latest in engines, communications, and targeting equipment. When the Kiowa happens to be the D model, the team is one

A Cobra uses terrain masking for cheap armor while executing a "cav" mission somewhere in deepest, darkest Fort Ord, California. The rotor wash kicks up dust and dirt, something to be avoided when you're trying to remain invisible.

A scrawny little AH-1 Cobra departs on a mission without mercy. The tandem layout for the crew makes the aircraft slightly more than shoulder width, a tiny target when you're thrashing around the sky at Warp Nine and the forces of evil are abroad in the land. *George Hall photo.*

of the most spectacularly capable systems in the air.

The Kiowa is another veteran of the Viet Nam War, an airframe that has been zipping through the blue for twenty plus years. Over there, it was a faithful artillery observer's seat in the sky. It worked well enough that the Army kept it longer than the soldiers who used it. But the old, familiar airframe contains a whole new set of systems, and the drivers of the Kiowa are quick to point out that the D model is an entirely different animal than the faithful Indian companion of yore. The latest version, the OH-58 D model, is considered one of the most capable aircraft in the American inventory, with a future that might last another twenty years. The reason is a synthesis of many technologies that makes the Delta froth at the mouth with pride.

Even if you compare the current Cobra with the Apache, the AH-1 is a hell of a machine. And it is available in vast numbers, serving all over the world with infantry and armor divisions that may never see an Apache. In fact, Cobra drivers (not the most impartial group, of course) think the Army made a big mistake by buying the Apache instead of just improving the faithful Cobra, as the Marines have done with their new twin-engine version.

The Cobra and the Apache both are capable of independent attack missions like the scenario used to open this book, but the day-to-day work of these aircraft is often more integrated into the ground commander's scheme of maneuver, and it fits right into the plan of battle used by light infantry, the airborne, and armored divisions. Air Cav uses helicopters in roles that once were (and still are) performed by men on foot, then later on horses, then in tanks and other vehicles. It essentially involves sending small numbers of quick, tough soldiers scurrying around the edges of the battlefield, particularly the flanks and out front, watching for the enemy. They are armed and trained to sting the enemy, not consume him. They are dangerous enough that they can't be taken lightly, weak enough to know when to run. The helicopter is designed to deliver a lot of different kinds of weapons, but when the TOW missile was adapted to be used on helicopters, it changed the way the Cobra was used and set the stage for the development of attack helicopter tactics. One pilot still in "guns" recalls the evolution of the Cobra mission from the early use as aerial artillery and spotting for the field artillery:

With the advent of the TOW, we suddenly had this tank-kill capability—and then the armor community was suddenly interested while the field artillery was not. Nobody used us as a maneuver element then; the idea was strictly (and still is today) "Guys, you support the folks on the ground and you don't do anything else; they don't want it, you don't do it." This has been called different things over the years, currently "combined arms"; there were lots of terms for that, but that's what it boiled down to.

But just recently, in the last few years, they've started to say, "Hey, we've got a tremendous amount of tank-kill capability here with the helicopters." In the late 1970s tank corps commanders began to say, "Jeeze, I've got all these brigades on line—if this huge horde comes and punches one of my brigades back, I can't move my reserve ground element around in there in time. But I can move my attack helicopters in there instantly! I'll use them like a maneuver brigade for breakthroughs," and they started thinking of us as a maneuver element. And that's where it has progressed, until now where we are a separate branch. Now everybody thinks of us as a maneuver element, and they're using us for all kinds of missions nobody ever considered before.

Typically, Cobras are teamed up with OH-58s and sent out to accomplish one of several kinds of mission, generally dependent on the kind of unit the aircraft and pilots come from. Attack helicopter units specialize in attack, antiarmor, joint air operations. Air Cav units specialize in surveillance, security, and recon missions. Both kinds of units can do the alternate type of mission, no mat-

ter how they are organized. How many of each machine depends on who wants to do what to whom. It's called "task organization." Two observation helicopters can be sent out for a recon mission when nobody really thinks the enemy is out there, but they want to look around anyway. But when contact with the opposing team is possible

---

If tankers ever see the helicopters that kill them, it will be visions like this: a Cobra unmasks from the Rockpile at the National Training Center to fire TOW missiles into attacking armor. The tank can kill the Cobra if he shoots first — but he has to see the target to hit it.

or expected, the commander will probably team an attack helicopter (Apache or Cobra) with an observation helicopter. He can even combine a gunship with an observer and a troop-carrying Black Hawk when you want to establish an OP or secure some essential real estate. It's possible to mix and match like crazy, because the attack platoons generally have three Kiowas and five Cobras to play with, while the Air Cav units have five Kiowas and three Cobras.

These are essentially the same missions that units on the ground may perform, and often

The gunner on this AH-1 Cobra sees the world through his telescopic sight unit (TSU) and everything is a target. The TSU has a wide 3 power field for searching and a 12 power narrow view for "putting steel downrange." The sight is gyro-stabilized, which eliminates most of the vibration of the aircraft. *George Hall photo.*

enough the helicopters use the same tried and true movement and engagement techniques that tanks and troops use: movement to contact, bounding overwatch, and so forth. Air Cav gives a task force (TF) commander a special kind of mobility and shock effect unavailable otherwise.

When coordinated with the ground forces, the commander's ability to see and influence the battlefield is tremendously increased by extensive and flexible radio communications. The flexibility of air and ground forces operating together makes it harder for an enemy to react. Air Cav can fulfill the attack role if it has to, but it is normally used for recon and security.

Since both the Cobra and Kiowa are vulnerable to enemy action, crews of both systems have polished their tactical skills to a high gloss. They are highly skilled at flying at night, and they don't just skim the tops of the trees; they fly below the treetops.

When a ground unit, like an armored brigade, plans a movement to contact with the enemy, a regimental commander will send the Air Cav troop out to recon the possible routes to advance and keep his attack companies in reserve, prepared to attack with the heavy punch.

We'll fly a typical mission in one of the latest versions of the Cobra, the F model, called the fully modernized Cobra because so many of its systems are upgraded, including the engine, weapons and fire control systems, a nose-mounted telescopic sight unit (the TSU), articulated pylons for the weapons stores on the winglets, an infrared (IR) jammer and suppressor, an airborne laser tracker, and an airspeed indicator that works in any direction.

Strapping into the front seat of a Cobra isn't all that different from stuffing yourself into any other helicopter; they're all a little awkward to mount. You learn to enter one the way you learn a new dance step; you've got to think about it the first few times, then it's automatic. The Cobra's cockpit is cozy compared to that of the bulkier cargo and utility airframes, but that's part of the idea.

When the helicopter was designed, it was with the expectation that it would be a target for people on the ground, so it is as small and narrow as an airframe can be while still carrying around all those guns, rockets, grenades, and two pilots. The front seater is called a "copilot gunner" (CPG). There is a full set of controls up there, and the CPG can drive if the back seater is not feeling well. The tandem layout makes for a very skinny target for somebody on the ground, and having you in the gunner's seat up front means I've got just a little extra armor between me and the bad guys if they should manage to hit us. Nice to have you along!

In front of the gunner are the controls for the weapons systems and the sights for them as well as a set of flight controls in case the pilot gets shot. There is a "head-up display" (HUD), which we use for lining up the aircraft when we fire rockets and the 20mm when it's in its fixed forward position. The TOW tubes, rockets, and ammunition storage compartment are each chock full of a nice mix of stuff to hunt the bad news bears. The full load of weapons means our fuel will be limited, so we're not going to be gone too long. Please keep your hands off the controls till we're out of the pattern.

We'll go out on a route recon today with one of the OH-58 D models, checking out a road the TF commander wants to use in a few hours. A route recon is a quick, cheap way for the boss to see if he'd likely to get ambushed when he sends a couple of brigades of armor through there tomorrow. He'd *much* rather lose us than a brigade of armor.

Every landscape can be a battlefield, every battlefield imposes limitations on the people who want to use it. We are going to see if the enemy is installing obstacles, digging in armor, deploying

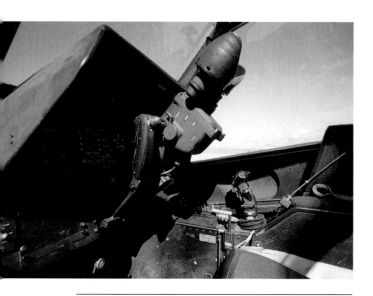

The front cockpit of a Cobra. The TSU is surrounded by flight and weapons systems controls. The gunner can fly or shoot but not usually both at the same time. The Cobra, unlike the Apache, requires the gunner to keep his head down—sometimes an advantage, sometimes not.

The pilot's gunsight on an AH-1 Cobra is similar to the head up display (HUD) found on Air Force attack aircraft. It allows the backseater to engage targets with guns or rockets while maneuvering the aircraft.

infantry, or anything else to prepare for an encounter with us. Our mission is to provide security for the OH-58, with its excellent sensor systems. We won't shoot unless we have to or have a good target of opportunity. The information we can provide is worth a lot more than anything we can kill by ourselves.

Since you are in the gunner's seat, it's your job to continuously hunt for targets. Keep your head down and watch the world go by through the telescopic sight unit. The TSU is a pretty amazing chunk of glass; it gives you two visions of the universe, a wide field and a narrow one, at the flip of a switch on your left-hand grip. Even at the high magnification, the image is smooth and free of vibration. Your right hand goes on the sight hand

control, fingers on the little metal rod, the "track stick." This rod doesn't move, but it does respond to pressure, so you can push against it and the sight picture will move in the same direction.

A gunner keeps his head down and all his fingers busy. There are switches for magnification; to arm the weapons; to select guns, rockets, or missiles; to operate the laser range finder/designator. But all the switches depend on input from the TSU, so you've got to be good with it, and that means smooth and steady. With the TSU optics set to LO, the sight reveals a 28-degree slice of the visual pie; you can slew the sight quickly over there to the ten o'clock position. I think I see a tank out there to the left; there's a little switch by your right pinky finger; move it to

ACQ, for acquire. See it? Okay, now switch to HI and you get a 4.6-degree view of the world, with a Soviet-built T-80 tank right there in the cross hairs, with "bad news" written all over him. He's moving left to right and seems to be "buttoned up" and alone, both of which make life easier for us and harder for him. It's hard to see out of a tank when the hatches are closed, and tanks normally work in teams for self protection.

With a little practice it is quite easy to put moving targets in the cross hairs and track them from several miles away, and that's what you've got to do now. It is easy to become absorbed in the process; the sight picture can become the gunner's private little world, and chasing targets at extreme ranges can be a fascinating game. But I think we ought to duck behind this ridge for a moment, because we are definitely in the enemy's range, and he's in ours.

A pair of 70mm folding fin rockets dash off into the gathering night to do their duty two miles downrange.

The TOW missile panel functions pretty much automatically, selecting a new missile as each is fired and displaying the remaining supply. The gunner can select them manually if any fail or are damaged by (gulp) ground fire.

When we in a helicopter start mixing it up with armor, we play a dangerous game. The tank has a gun that can usually hit us at the same ranges that we can hit him. We try to shoot targets that are in the last third of the range of the weapons system, and for the TOW, that means about two and a half klicks away. We'll unmask for a moment to let you lase the tank with the laser range finder. The little window reveals a distance of 2,755 meters — just about right. Above the sight is the TOW control panel, and if you rotate the MODE SELECT switch to AUTO ARMED, we will be "good to go."

The fire control computer (FCC) and the sophisticated nature of the missile will do a lot for you, but not everything. You've got to be careful or you'll waste several thousand dollars worth of missile, plus perhaps the chance to survive to shoot another. Anyway, it takes both hands, thirty seconds, and a functional brain to get the missile from A to B. We'll unmask again; quickly reacquire the target, first at LO power until you get it in the inner sight circle, then at HI. There is a small bar on the inside of the left handgrip; press it with your left pinky and you get an attack flag in the sight reticule, meaning the FCC has selected a missile and is ready to turn it loose.

Keep tracking the target with the cross hairs on the "center of mass" while I maneuver the helicopter to get it "in constraints," which means pointed generally at the target for launch. As soon as the FCC approves of my flying, an X disappears from my HUD and you get a bright R for "ready" in the TSU. Use your left index/trigger finger to squeeze the trigger, and a flash of flame streaks away from our left weapons pylon. The first of our ten TOWs departs on its mission, and if the bad guys are paying any attention, they should be trying to acquire us. And they'll have plenty of time to do just that, because it will take about twenty seconds for the TOW to reach from here to there, and we have to track it every second. Their gun, however, can easily clean us out of the sky first; its projectile can arrive less than a second after it leaves their tube, so the first round better work and we need to be lucky.

The TOW missiles are rather individual beasts, some being more responsive than others, so you need to test each one soon after it leaves. They all like to wander a bit, a couple of feet from the line of sight you give it through the two little wires that trail out the back, so you've got to be as precise as you can throughout the flight. Although the TSU will stay pointed in the same direction

despite any maneuvering of the helicopter, I still have to keep the Cobra pointed in the direction of the target (in constraints). If we get out of constraints, I'll have wasted the missile for you.

The TSU and FCC provide all the help they can. When the action bar is depressed at the same time you move the sights with the target, the TSU will maintain this rate for you, which is handy when the target disappears behind trees, for example. But you still have to be careful to apply smooth, quick corrections and keep the cross

This backseater scans for targets but won't be able to shoot at anything over there until he turns the helicopter. The aircraft has to be maneuvered to point in the general direction of the target before missiles or guns can be fired.

hairs centered until — IMPACT! Nice shot; let's get the hell out of here.

Well, that was a lucky engagement, and hopefully we won't have to do that very often. Heavy armor is getting too dangerous for TOWs, and we can let the Apaches fight the hard-core opposition because of their greater standoff range. The

Cobra's systems are still good, though, for light armor, bunkers, point targets, and—yuk—air-defense artillery positions. We shine as an escort for an observation helicopter, which is why the Cobra is such a great asset for cavalry outfits, with their emphasis on mobility and flexibility rather than brute firepower. Although we're more of a day system than the Apache, we still do a lot of work at night with night vision goggles. We're dangerous enough to the enemy that we can screen and scout if we're careful about it.

APACHE

The AH-64 Apache attack helicopter is a special system and it attracts special people. It is designed to be one thing—an industrial-strength battlefield killing machine.

The Apache is new and expensive, and has received a lot of attention in the media, so let's take a close look and see what the excitement is all about. Out on the flight line, the AH-64 Apache looks mean even with the blades tied down. Maybe it's the little winglets with their missile racks and rocket pods, or the 30mm gun hanging below the nose. It's a big airframe for an attack helicopter, but it has to be big to carry all those weapons and the computers required to make them work. The Apache has the reach and punch to hit hard before it can be hit itself and can risk some direct attack missions, a capability that

The Apache takes the Cobra concept farther down the road. More power and better sights mean a much bigger gun, a much better missile, plus the same load of 70mm rockets can be carried faster, farther, in more adverse conditions than before. *George Hall photo.*

has made it the star of Army aviation for the moment.

The AH-64 is the most complicated and ambitious system the Army has ever fielded, an aerial version of the M1 tank, but costing about six times more. It is supposed to work on the darkest night, in rain, fog, snow, and sleet, in the dust and confusion of the battlefield. It is designed to detect targets at extreme ranges, and engage more than one at a time. It is expected to kill the best armor an enemy can offer, and kill a lot of it; then it is expected to survive and be able to fight again.

When not killing armor, the Apache gets other demanding missions. One of these is to provide a "covering force" that detects and slows an attacker before it can reach the main body of friendly troops. Another is "flank security," in which the helicopter patrols the vulnerable edges of a force, insuring that the enemy is unable to surprise friendly units. Then there is "economy of force," which uses small forces—like a few helicopters—in strategic locations, freeing ground units to mass on decisive terrain. As a supreme gunship, the Apache makes for an excellent airmobile escort, protecting the vulnerable lift helicopters as they provide taxi service for the troops headed into battle. The Apache can use its tremendous volume of firepower and accurate delivery for area suppression missions, taking out air defense artillery (ADA) and other defenses prior to an assault. While all these missions are older than the helicopter, the Apache has been designed to do them with speed, flexibility, and effectiveness under conditions that used to shut down other systems. These missions couldn't be done until developments in technology made them possible, and the Apache is a black box helicopter.

The Apache is designed to work close to the terrain, using it for cover and concealment. Everybody expects the next war to be fought with sophisticated weapons, with lots of radar and infrared systems used by an enemy against U.S. aircraft. These weapons are dangerous, but can be defeated, and flying very low helps. The Apache can hide behind a hill, a technique called "masking," and then "unmask" just long enough to shoot. When there's another helicopter or ground designator around, the Apache doesn't even have to see its target; a "handoff" is all that's required. Someone else can actually put the laser spot on the tank turret, insuring an accurate hit and an Apache that will get back to the reservation.

The Apache carries up to sixteen Hellfire missiles, and it doesn't need to shoot them singly. It can turn loose several and then identify their targets in sequence, rapidly taking out a lot of tanks. The fire control computer can handle up to ten targets at once and keep track of them for the convenience of the gunner.

Army aviation has never really seen anything like the Apache, and the community is still trying to get used to the idea of a helicopter that can be rolled. There are pictures on the bulletin boards of the beast quite completely upside down, and you're not supposed to be able to do that! Of course, rolling helicopters, while fun, is also dangerous, so it is not permitted.

The Apache is a very impressive system, when everything is working right: better than 160 knots indicated airspeed (KIAS) in level flight, 45 knots sideways or backwards, a rate of climb of 3,000 feet per minute, able to take 3.5 positive g's, and a maximum gross weight (with external fuel tanks) of 21,000 pounds. That makes it very light on its feet, even when carrying a full load of goodies.

If we walk around the AH-64 Apache and do a

preflight inspection, it's obvious that there are some things about this helicopter that are different from the others, starting with the paint. The AH-64 Apache has a special, expensive, IR-absorbing paint that is supposed to make it harder for enemy systems to see. In fact, special paint is just one of the several countermeasures used on the aircraft as part of the life insurance policies the Army is buying for its helicopters; two others are a radar jammer that works automatically and an infrared jammer designed to drive heat-seeking missiles nuts. There are also four little

disks mounted around the helicopter, little antennas for the APR radar detector that tells you somebody is watching.

In the cockpit you can sit up front in the gunner's seat or in back where the pilot works. Both can fly the helicopter and both can use the weapons. A thick glass panel separates the front from the back, and although you can see through it, the

Every flight hour requires several hours of grooming by the faithful enlisted mechanics, one of whom is making sure the Apache's blades are still screwed on tight. *George Hall photo.*

Before slipping the surly bonds of earth it is a good idea to review the checklist and the map. *George Hall photo*.

laminate will stop a big bullet. The designers expected that the AH-64 Apache was going to be shot at a lot out in the real world, and they designed it so that both the helicopter and the crew would be protected as much as possible. There is a lot of armor around your seat and elsewhere on the Apache. The blades can take hits from heavy machine guns and continue to fly for hours. The gearboxes and other drivetrain components are also supposed to be able to shrug off a lot of hits that would be fatal for earlier helicop-

ters. All this protection adds a lot of weight, and the Apache is a heavy helicopter; but with two engines it can lose one and still stand a chance of completing its mission and getting back home.

The individual systems are designed to be easy to use, and they are, one at a time. But when a task force commander has asked you to help with some little chore on a dark and stormy night, with the forces of evil abroad in the land, all those user-friendly systems begin to demand 101 percent of your mental capacity. But you don't want to hear about it, you want to try it. Let's go hunting for bear.

For such a big, expensive airplane, the AH-64 Apache is easy to start. The SOP in and out of the Army is to use the checklist to carefully preflight the aircraft and then to set the switches and controls before flight to make sure nothing gets broken, including you. With the preflight done, we're ready to go for a ride. You can tell which switches get used—they're the shiny ones. All the switches are in the correct positions, so now we pull the pin that safeties the explosive canopy jettison system in case we want to bail out. Turn on the battery; test the warning systems to see if any "chiclets" are burned out on the engine instru-

An Apache lives and works close to the soldiers that it supports. This Apache is being field-refuelled from jerry cans. *George Hall photo.*

ment display; then over on the MASTER CAUTION panel, press the PRESS TO TEST button, and they all light up.

There is an automatic bore sight procedure to align the laser with the weapons sights systems. Just before we pop the brakes we turn the HARS (stability augmentation system) to OPERATE and we're ready to go.

Now for some magic: there's a little television screen right in the middle of the panel, and the programs you can see on it are fascinating and educational in the extreme. The "dash 10" calls it the video display unit, but AH-64 Apache drivers just call it the VDU. You can use it several ways, and can slave to the other guys' display or use it to look in another direction or at some different kind of information. When you've got on the HMD and the pilot night vision system (PNVS), you can see the PNVS display in your right eye at the same time you can look at the CPG's video, just like changing channels on Saturday morning but with real-life Dudley Doright and Boris Badinoff.

Apache drivers get a special $15,000 helmet, and though it may look a little funny, try not to laugh, because in this case looks can kill. Behind each seat are four little black boxes that project a pattern of light in the cockpit; each helmet has two sets of reflectors designed to work with the boxes. Once you calibrate the system, it can tell exactly where your eyes are looking, which would be no big deal except that here the guns can be slaved to your line of sight. By looking at a target (and having the switches in the right positions), you can aim the gun at it. And, coupled with the helmet mounted display (HMD), you can keep track of your other systems at the same time, even while looking over your shoulder. The HMD is really just a tiny television screen, only about an inch across, and its tiny image reflects off a partial mirror in front of your right eye. The actual image is only about an eighth of an inch across, but when you've got the helmet on and the HMD is attached and focused, a bright green image is superimposed wherever you look. Using a minimum of lines and symbols, the display can show you your magnetic heading, the direction you should fly to your next way point, rate of climb and airspeed, missile constraints, radar altitude, rocket steering cursor, hover position, artificial horizon, engine torque, and a lot of other things only a pilot could care about. But basically it keeps both crew members fully informed all the time about the aircraft status, navigation information, and weapons systems, regardless of how hot the action may be or how dark the night.

The IHADS and HMD are really only data inputs to that most amazing computer of all, the Army aviator, who has the mission of delivering tremendous amounts of firepower under extremely adverse conditions. He does his work with no more than the press of a button and a flick of a switch, but to be successful, the button has to be pressed at a very precise moment in a complicated scenario. That's what the black boxes are for.

One of the senior IPs evaluates the Apache and its missions:

I like the airframe, engine, rotor, performance of this aircraft better than any I've ever flown, by far. It will just do so much for me. You can't argue with results. It will out-maneuver any other aircraft; we don't know how much air-to-air we'll be doing officially, but we better get there quick. The Soviets have a couple of helicopters in production that would be a problem for us air-to-air, but

right now we're the most maneuverable gunship around. As with any A-model aircraft, it's got a lot of bugs to work out, and we're the primary work-outers right here in this company; we fly more hours in Apaches than anybody in the United States Army. So it's a bit of a nuisance to go through the growing pains of an A model; by the time we get up to a T model this thing is going to be fine! I'm not personally pleased with its reliability so far on the high-tech end of it. As far as the basic helicopter goes, it's fine right now, but

Capt. Rick Rife, Gremlin Six, scans the terrain at eleven o'clock for targets and obstacles while cruising along at 120 knots and a 20-foot altitude. Sensors on the bulkhead behind him "read" the position of his helmet and tell the computer where he is looking.

the black boxes are a problem. The FLIR system is capable of performing its mission, but only with very highly trained operators. Great airframe; flies good! And the avionics and the weapons delivery systems, when they work, are just excellent. And it crashes good, too! We've had some of the major crashes here, and I've had a chance to walk through the wreckage afterwards and see what broke and what didn't. If you can hit the ground right side up in this thing, you can probably walk away from the crash. It has a tremendous capability to absorb vertical g's. So far as combat survivability goes, we don't know yet, but there is certainly a lot of intention to make it tolerate all sorts of damage. We don't know yet—but we'll find out! If they said: "You must crash—pick your airplane," I'll take an Apache.

This thing is designed to kill tanks, that's its forte. With the range capability and the laser designator, it's awesome! We can kill tanks when the tank doesn't have a prayer of touching us. We can stay so far out of his range he can do nothing about it. That's nice. With the TOW you had to get at least inside his range and occasionally inside his effective range, and that's not so nice. So, from a tank kill capability, there is nothing better on the battlefield—as far as aircraft—than the Apache.

Cross FLOT, deep raids, high-risk missions like that I'm personally not big on because I've seen what happens too many times—and it ain't fun! As a division or a corps commander, the moment you make the decision to send us 60 or 80 kilometers deep, even in a medium-threat environment, what you've done is throw a spear . . . and it's not coming back to you. It's gone! If the target was worth throwing that spear at, you did good. But your spear is not coming back, or if it is, it's coming back in pieces. That's the way I look at deep strike, and there are people who will

This Apache is a little high for a wartime excursion, but in training power lines kill a lot more pilots than bullets do, especially at twilight. *George Hall photo.*

argue with me and say we can get in and back in one piece. I believe it will be a rare situation where that's true. So if the target is lucrative enough and you are willing to expend the asset to get it, get it. If not, my feeling is: try another way. I know there are situations where nothing will do but men in cockpits, but they are so rare, let's not waste Apaches on missions that could just as easily be done with artillery or long-range missiles.

KIOWA

The OH-58 in its Delta model configuration is making quite an impression on people in the Army, on the ground, and in the air. An instructor pilot (IP) from the Army Aviation Center at Fort Rucker tells why:

The OH-58 D is quite possibly the finest aircraft the Army has come up with in the last twenty years. It's got the best communications equipment in the Army, stabilized optics better than any pair of binoculars, and its almost invisible small size makes it easy to hide, and it's fast enough to do the job. Army tactics today don't emphasize speed, they emphasize stealth, and that's what we do. It's a wonderful aircraft, better at night than during the day.

The crucial difference between my aircraft and any other in the inventory is that I don't have to unmask to see the target. All I have to reveal is that little two-foot ball on top of the mast. We've sat for 45 minutes with nothing but that ball poking over the hill, and nobody knows you're there. From any more than a couple of hundred meters you just can't see that ball.

· The pilot can do the work that used to be done by two people thanks to the MFD [multifunction display]. That means the observer is free to concentrate on acquiring targets and dealing with them.

The Delta model can't be mistaken for any other helicopter, even though its basic lines are those of Bell Helicopter's popular Jet Ranger. The OH-58 is the military version of that design, and the earlier A and C models were not much different from the civilian aircraft, other than the paint job and radios. But the D model is a fundamentally different beast, even though the family resemblance is strong. And this has turned out to be a real problem for the IPs who teach the new system to pilots who've flown the old one for any length of time. It may look like the old aircraft, but it is a totally new system and some people have trouble adjusting.

The OH-58 is good for about 125 KIAS with the doors on, 100 off. It will carry only two people, the back end now crammed with black boxes and wires. There are four blades instead of two, and perched right in the middle of them is a big green sphere; even when the rotors are turning, this ball is stationary. The crews call it the "beach ball," and although it's the same size as one, please don't go tossing it around because it costs about a million dollars—and when it's doing its job, it's priceless. The beach ball is the key to many of the unique capabilities of the Delta, part of a system the Army calls the mast-mounted sight (MMS).

The 58 D doesn't normally carry weapons of its own, and it shouldn't need them. Its laser designator can bring down the wrath of what will seem like God on whoever is painted with its coded light. All sorts of "smart" munitions are designed to seek out and land on this special kind of laser light, including bombs from the Air

Force, "Copperhead" artillery rounds fired from the 155mm howitzers, and the Hellfire missile. All the crew has to do, in essence, is point at something and make the "call for fire."

The MMS is most of the foundation of the Delta, and when the sophisticated radios and computers are linked to the MMS, the pilot and the enlisted observer can do really amazing things. "We've been able to acquire and identify rabbits at a thousand meters on a totally dark night," one pilot says. That is a long distance for

An OH-58C Kiowa from the 82d Airborne Division hides out for a few minutes in a little clearing not far from the battle. The C model and the new D are both based on the rugged, reliable Bell Jet Ranger air frame that has been around for longer than most of its pilots.

a small target. Other systems in the past might have been able to acquire it—to know something was there—but not be able to tell what it was.

The 58 is both easier and more difficult to use compared to the older model observation helicopters. Flying it is easy; the basics put a far

An instructor pilot from the Army Aviation Center sports AN/PVS night vision goggles. Behind him, in what used to be a backseat, is a mass of radios, computers, and navigation equipment that have transformed the aircraft and its mission. The Delta has a crew of two, the pilot and an enlisted sensor operator.

lower workload on the pilot. But all those black boxes and the MMS mean it can do a great deal more, so the crews are expected to accomplish more. There are radios that can talk to the Air Force and Navy, as well as the usual Army equipment. "We have four radios, and there are times when I can be using all four at the same time, while working with the Air Force," says one IP.

The helicopter astounds its students with its power and performance: it can hover out of ground effect at 6,000 feet when the air tempera-

ture is 112 degrees — and that's thin air. The power reserve makes it strong and agile, able to maneuver quickly, dashing from one covered and concealed position to another. One of the instructors at Rucker comments:

I LOVE the aircraft! I don't want to fly anything

else! You can detect targets at extreme ranges, navigate from one point to another without ever picking up a map—and arrive within twenty or thirty meters of a grid coordinate after traveling great distances. When I get there, I don't have to guess about how far away my targets are; with the systems on board I can get an eight-digit grid coordinate of that location. We can send that data back to an artillery unit to "service" the target; we can send it as a one-second data burst, digitally encoded, instead of the old thirty-second messages that revealed us to the enemy. The actual

mission of the aircraft is to go out in the trees and hunt targets, and it's great!

The primary mission for the 58 is supposed to be target acquisition for the field artillery, handing off targets to the big guns. But because of its capability, it's used to do more than that. Now, most often the 58 will work with one or more

---

The Kiowa at a low hover. While wider than a gunship, the OH-58 is still a pretty small target, particularly when it's playing hide and seek through the treetops.

gunships, and it will hand off its targets to an Apache or Cobra, which then "service" the target with missiles or rockets. Sometimes they'll work with the Air Force, especially during wartime. Another instructor sums up the capabilities of the Delta:

We've got two "fox-mike" [FM], a VHF and a UHF radio means we can talk to anybody, and we can do digital data transmission over any of them. When we work with the artillery, the combination of the highly accurate nav system, the stabilized optics, and the laser designator means that we can provide exact locations for targets in excess of nine thousand meters. Out in the desert when we've worked with the Air Force, we acquire targets at twenty kilometers and identify them at nine kilometers where we can designate them for attack by F-16s. Doctrine seems to be changing from artillery support to more of a cav role, and there is one unit in the Army that uses the 58 as an attack helicopter.

That one unit he mentions (and is careful to say no more about) is doing its training in the Persian Gulf, and the bad guys are not just playing games. The Army doesn't have much to say about this unit, but the rumor mill indicates that these 58s are working closely with the Navy and Air Force, and that they are equipped with Stinger air-to-air missiles and Hellfires. The Kiowas are Deltas but with any of several kinds of weapons linked to the MMS. This configuration is called the "Warrior," and can shoot four Hellfires or Stingers (for air to air), machine guns, or the new Hydra 70 rockets with any of several warheads. The reason for using the 58 instead of an Apache or Cobra is the combination of radios and the incredibly capable MMS, which together with the weapons provides a commander (even a Navy commander) with a resource that can see and shoot at threats that were safe before.

A common mission sends out one or two 58s with a gunship for protection. When targets are designated and the "call for fire" is made, it is usually fire for effect on the first round. If the gun crew is good at its business, the first round ought to hit within a hundred meters of the target, because the precision of the 58's systems is so good. All the technologies of the Delta are out front. It sends spot reports and status reports in a digital format, with automatic features only a pilot could love. Instead of talking on the radio, the crew can send the most important messages almost instantaneously, and they show up on a screen instead of in a headset. This not only preserves messages in computer memory for later reference, it also allows a constant log of the positions of other aircraft. If you take ground fire and go down, the system lets you send off an automatic and instantaneous Mayday that only the friendly side can hear. That Mayday will include your present position, accurate to a hundred meters.

The system is so capable that it has taken awhile for the Army to believe it. One IP who helped test the new model had a hard time getting his information accepted: "I helped test the prototype, and we could get targets beyond the design specs of the systems—so we didn't get credit because the computer evaluating the data wasn't programmed for such extreme ranges. But we could see exactly where they were, when they were coming, sit there and count them and send that real-time information back to the commander so he can make his plans as early as possible." Another pilot describes a trip to the National Training Center (NTC), where armored

The multifunction display (MFD) is the key to the new role for the OH-58. The MFD can show highly accurate navigation data, aircraft flight information, a stabilized daytime television view, and a clear thermal image of the terrain on the darkest night.

A scout/gunship team scoot, snoop, and communicate—the traditional role of the cavalry since the days of horses and before. The Cobra's mission is to protect the vulnerable OH-58, which is toothless, in the unfortunate event of a brawl.

units slug it out in the most realistic training the Army can offer. Aviation is busy at NTC, where the wide open spaces are really wide, and the visibility is extreme. Even so, TF commanders had a hard time believing the reports the Deltas were providing. "The first day's reports were so precise that the planners didn't want to believe that our data wasn't at least partially invented; the second day they started matching the spot reports from the scouts with the engagement reports, and noticed that they looked awfully similar—and by the third day, if a 58 didn't fly, they didn't go."

Working cooperatively with other kinds of systems is a big part of what the Delta is supposed to do, and it is becoming a hot topic throughout the military. Target handoff is the key: one system acquires, identifies, and designates a target—a tank, for example—and another weapons system uses the data from the first to "service" it. It's called ATHS, for automatic target handoff system, and will be featured on American tanks and attack aircraft. One pilot says:

I just did a demonstration with Air Force A-10s with the "Pave Penny" pod, but dropping dumb iron bombs. All I had to do was be out in the target area on the right frequency and when the A-10 called "in-bound" I just lased the target with the code I was given. It was 4,500 meters away, a pretty good distance for what we're used to; I heard him say he had the spot, then saw him maneuver on the target and release his bomb. He called "outbound" and the target in my cross hairs blew up. The amount of cooperation was minimal and the bomb wasn't even a precision weapon; I never even talked to the guy. I just lased the target, he dropped the bomb and left, and I left.

Beans and Bullets
— Chinook

"This is the best aircraft the Army's got," says the W4 pilot with the 1st Air Cav combat patch on his right shoulder, and he should know because he's been flying all of them for twenty years. He's sitting in the right seat of a Delta model CH-47 Chinook on the ramp at Hanchey Army Airfield at Fort Rucker. He has logged hundreds of combat sorties in Viet Nam, earning dozens of Air Medals in the process, plus one Purple Heart. Now he's got a really scary mission: he teaches young warrant officer candidates how to fly the big Chinook.

All pilots have favorite aircraft, and most are partial to the one they fly now and say nasty things about all other helicopters and the people who fly them. The pilot sits back, comfortable and at home in a multimillion-dollar extension of himself. He will be retiring soon, but the aircraft will continue to work for the Army for another decade or two. In fact the Chinook has reenlisted in the form of a new generation, the D model, and will be around into the twenty-first century, providing the ground pounders with combat support and combat service support, as it has been for decades.

The rumor that the Chinook prototype was actually a White Freightliner truck is only partly true. The designers at Boeing did not simply take the wheels off and put the rotors and engines on one of those eighteen wheelers, but it's close. The big CH-47 is a kind of airborne truck, a large cargo compartment able to accept just about any-thing and take it just about anywhere, a design tried and tested in war and peace for nearly three decades and still going strong. It is really just a box that flies. The wheels are smaller than the truck's, and it certainly costs more, but then it will go all sorts of places a truck cannot.

The CH-47 was part of the new generation of helicopters developed during the middle and late 1950s around the capabilities of the then-new gas turbine engine; it started joining the inventory in 1963 as a medium-lift helicopter. Like any new design, the Chinook had its share of teething problems, and when it was time for the 1st Air Cav to go off to war, the A-model Chinooks needed more than a thousand little modifications before they could leave. Once in the Central Highlands, though, the Chinooks did yeoman's service, moving people and equipment from place to place right over the heads of the VC. The Chinook is a big target and took a lot of hits; many were lost. Armor was added, which helped, at least sometimes. But the thing that really pleased the old helicopter drivers from the piston era was its power. In a pinch you could fill up the cargo compartment with all the Viet-namese you could jam in there (I've heard rumors of 127) and still get off the ground and back to the barn. Sure, you might go over the "never exceed" gross weight, but there were times when the hills were alive with the sound of gunfire and you didn't care what the "dash 10" said.

During the war in Viet Nam, people with a sense of adventure and ingenuity tried bolting all sorts of weapons to the Chinook, including rockets and .50-caliber machine guns, but the beast was never cut out to be an attack helicopter. Instead, it was the foundation for a variety of suc-cessful innovations, one of which was the use of

A Special Forces (Green Beret) A team demonstrates an insertion technique called "fast rope" with the help of the 160th Aviation Brigade's fully tricked out Chinook D model. The Chinook can carry huge loads deep into Indian country, navigating with tremendous precision.

a long ladder to insert troops into 200-foot-tall jungle canopy and recover them. The technique involved a long, light ladder as wide as the helicopter's ramp, made of cables and cross members. By lowering this contraption through the canopy, troops could climb down into areas that were previously inaccessible. Of course the ladder could have been used with any utility or cargo helicopter, but it took the Chinook's tremendous power to hover in the high, hot air with a load aboard.

There are still a few A-model Chinooks left, but they are returning to their birthplace to be transformed into even more capable D models. The Deltas are rated to 50,000 pounds gross weight, and with three cargo hooks they can easily sling the huge 155mm howitzer, a truck, a "gamma-goat" tactical utility vehicle and trailer, or a huge pallet of ammunition.

The D-model Chinook is a remarkable part of the mix of Army aviation, but in order to really appreciate the aircraft, we should fly it, so let's go.

We're with the 82d Airborne Division today, down in some steamy Caribbean island nation defending the forces of democracy against the forces of evil. The 82d has already jumped in and secured the airhead, and the second echelon has been delivered courtesy of the USAF. The Chinooks have come in giant C-5A transports, blades folded, and delivered to a secure staging field on a nearby island. Blades are swiftly replaced, and it isn't long until the Chinooks are ready to go to work.

If you have never flown in an earlier Chinook, it's difficult to fully appreciate the elegance and simplicity of the D model's front office. The old arrays of gauges and controls have been replaced by a big screen in front of each seat. This one screen, on command, displays all you need to know and more about where you are, where you're going, and the health of the beastie that's taking you there. The latest in nav systems lets you enter the grid coordinates of your destination, the place you want to call home, and all your navigational way points in between. You can go from point A to point B with the greatest of ease and precision, thanks to the expensive black boxes behind the bulkhead. You can almost fly the whole thing hands off, but don't try it.

We'll be supporting elements of the 325th Parachute Infantry Regiment, who are methodically enlarging the airhead and fighting small, well-organized groups of insurgents and regulars. The enemy is using noncombatant civilians for cover and concealment, so it is a cautious, careful advance. The bad guys have excellent Soviet-made weapons, including AK-74s, RPGs, Sagger missiles, and occasional multibarreled antiaircraft guns—all of which can bring us down. But it will be safer where we are going than it is forward where the Apaches and Cobras are working.

At our briefing at a very casual TOC, we are told what we'll be lifting today. It will be a real mixed bag: we'll start with an artillery raid; then a platoon of aerorifle scouts will be dropped out in the boonies; and finally, we'll resupply a battalion with food, water, and ammunition. Then we'll see what else they want us to do.

Like most other Army helicopters, you start the Chinook by first lighting off a little auxiliary power unit, a small gas turbine that supplies electrical and hydraulic power to start the main engines. The start sequence is simple, and we use the checklist to insure that we don't inadvertently damage anything: APU START switch to START,

Back to the barn for an old C model and its time-tested crew from the 140th Aviation Company, a Guard outfit. The reserves and Guard are in many ways more capable than the active duty units, their crews often having thousands of hours of flying—many with combat tours in Viet Nam.

The front office of the Charlie model 47 hasn't changed much in 25 years, but when this old soldier goes back to the factory it will emerge as a transformed Delta model. The cockpit will sport multipurpose displays instead of the old gauges.

First class accommodations in the Chinook come with seats; the economy section sits on the deck. Nobody smokes and the stewardess isn't cute, but the travelers get guided tours in some exotic locations. And, on this luxury liner, it's okay to bring along guns and grenades.

and from the back of the box comes the delicious rising pitch of the little turbine as it spins up to speed. Then, with a little whoosh, it lights off automatically, and the pitch increases and grows louder as it comes to life, warms up, and starts putting out power. Our engine instruments show nice, healthy green chiclets, and it's time to fire up the number one engine.

Unlike the attack helicopters, which usually work together in teams, we will be operating solo today. Our grid coordinates go into the GPS NAV computer (GPS stands for global positioning system), and now the helicopter knows where we are to within 100 meters; the location of the artillery is also entered, and now the helicopter knows where we're going. Then we'll enter the grid num-

bers for the new location for the battery, and that's just about all we need. We'll carry maps, of course, but we shouldn't need them for basic navigation.

Okay, everything's in the green. Key the ICS on the cyclic with your trigger finger and make sure the flight engineer is set: "Ready in back?"

"Roger, good to go," is the reply from the sergeant, who checks for possible mechanical problems inside and for any unsafe conditions outside.

The CH-47 is so big and heavy that, when possible, we taxi away from other aircraft and vehicles to a takeoff spot. But here in the field that's not an option. Fortunately there are no tents within several hundred meters, and nothing else likely to be damaged, so we'll leave from here.

"Clear in back!" the NCO reports, and it's time to pull pitch.

Of all the aircraft in the Army inventory, the CH-47 is the only one that has a crew of three, one being an enlisted flight engineer. This is one of the most responsible positions available to noncommissioned officers in aviation. The pilots and flight engineer form a team of mutual inter-dependence, on the ground and in the air. If the flight engineer tells us there is a problem in flight and he wants us to put the helicopter on the ground, we'll park it first and ask questions later.

Come up on the collective and the helicopter gets light, rising up on those four little toes until the struts hit the stops and we're clear of the ground. The two rotor systems counterrotate, which means that the torque effects that make other helicopters nervous and squirrelly at a hover don't exist with the CH-47; that, plus its

As simple and elegant as a shoebox, the Chinook is a big, strong cargo container with two powerful gas turbine engines and a brilliant drive train/rotor design that has survived the test of time, bullets, and a multitude of missions on every continent and in every climate.

larger mass, makes it easier to hover, although it still takes a light touch to keep it on top of that cushion of compressed air without sliding around in an undignified manner. Up on the collective until we're about ten feet off the ground, then smoothly add forward cyclic and we begin to move forward, slowly at first, then faster. Keep adding collective and forward cyclic; the nose is down and we're pointed at the ground, although we're accelerating through forty KIAS as we clear the trees by a good fifty feet. Hi ho, hi ho, it's off to work we go!

One of the things that keeps life interesting for Chinook drivers is the tremendous diversity of things people want you to do for them. Take this first mission for example. We are going to collect a really big artillery piece, a 155mm howitzer so powerful that its maximum range is classified; then we are going to haul that gun *and* its ammunition *and* crew deep into enemy territory, put it down in range of some juicy targets, and wait while the "gun bunnies" service the targets. They'll fire just enough rounds to get the other team really annoyed, then they'll pack up their toys and expect us to take them home again. We will actually sit on the ground and wait for the gun crew to put their rounds in the air. We are going so deep into enemy territory that we'll bring along a "mother cow," another Chinook with a bladder of fuel, to refuel us, so we can get home. Before the big turbine helicopters came along, an artillery raid like this one just wasn't an option; but new technologies become new tactics as people imagine ways to apply them.

We'll stay down in the treetops for safety's sake, keeping about ten feet of clearance, and we will come up to 120 knots for the run into the artillery battalion pickup point. From such a low

One of the 82d Airborne's CH-47s comes up to a hover, ready to hook up to an external load of groceries and explosives. Light infantry units like the 82d will survive in combat only if the Chinook and its brethren do their duty and supply the troops with ammunition, water, MREs, and replacements.

altitude and at this speed, there are few terrain reference points to help us find our destination; but the GPS points the way, and soon we arrive at a little clearing like dozens of others in the area—except that this one has five howitzers lined up in it, nice and neat, with trailers and slings and crews waiting in breathless anticipation. One soldier stands conspicuously in the open, both arms raised in the universal helicopter signal: "guide on me!" He will position us above the loads and help us hook up. But first he'll bring us down to the ground to put the gun crews aboard.

We face him, nose to nose, and reduce speed until we are at a high hover 100 meters out. His arms come down now, and he motions us down and forward with the formal signals he learned in

Air Assault School and that we all know now by heart. As we get closer, our guide is sandblasted by the downwash. Goggles protect his eyes, but he still gets hit by the hundred-mile-per-hour blast of air until we get on the ground and can lower the collective.

The crew chief has the ramp down, and at our signal the gun crew rush aboard with their packs and weapons and are quickly seated and strapped in. Then we pick up again and the guide signals us over one of the guns. A soldier stands beside it with the sling loop in both hands, ready to endure the horrific downblast. As we slide over the top of the load, we can no longer see it and must rely on the crew chief and the ground guide for information. Since a mistake can squash a soldier and an aircraft, Chinook drivers tend to be artists of a high order when it comes to hovering. There is only a few feet of space where the sling and the cargo hook can meet, and the hookup man, buffeted by the blast, has an awkward job. It can be a painful one, too, because the tremendous charge of static electricity generated by those rotors will go right through him the first time he touches the aircraft if we have neglected to key the FM radio, which somehow dissipates the charge. The jolt can knock him right off the load.

We are soon latched securely to the first gun, and then to its trailer full of ammunition, and it is time to hit the road. The guide signals a solid hookup on the trailer and brings us up until it and the gun are both clear of the ground, then he

---

This is *not* fun. It is too noisy and windy, you get sand-blasted by the down wash, and if the bozo driving isn't careful you could get squished between the load and the helicopter. And if you don't hop off after the pickup you get a ride!

points to the sky and tells us to scram. With all that stuff dangling underneath, we shall scram in the indicated direction, but slowly and carefully, and not before pausing a moment for a hover power check to insure that we have enough power to handle the load and that the aircraft is acting normally at these high power settings. The little black boxes make the Chinook as maneuverable with a maximum gross weight load as an old A model was when empty; it can even handle a 60-degree angle of bank with a 155 howitzer underneath. Even unstable loads like Conex

Artillery is the biggest killer on the battlefield (no matter what the Air Force says) and moving it quickly from one place to a better one is a prime responsibility of the Chinook. The big 47 can easily tote the gun, its crew, and a lifetime supply of bullets.

boxes—previously a 30-knot cargo—can be rigged and flown at 120 knots.

Sling loading is a kind of minor art form, appreciated by a small and select group of critics. It has taken a long time to evolve, although the technique is as old as the cargo helicopter. The technique looks simple enough, but it can be complicated. The aerodynamic forces and center of gravity shift dramatically when you hang something heavy twenty or thirty feet below your normal center of gravity. Control movements have to be much more gradual and slow, and you have got to be glass smooth on your turns. The flight engineer is lying down in the back; he isn't asleep but watching through the hole in the floor to make sure the load is behaving itself. The consequences of misbehavior are very dangerous, as was demonstrated early in the history of the CH-47.

Shortly after the Chinook was fielded, in 1964, an attempt was made at Fort Benning to sling load the carcass of a CH-47 with major mechanical problems, the intention being to transport it to the depot maintenance facility near Atlanta. A drogue parachute was attached to the load to stabilize it in flight, the hookup was made, and

This reserve crew and helicopter have both war and peace missions. The latter were tested after the California earthquake of 1989 when the 140th's Chinooks helped with the massive rescue effort.

The external load capability of cargo helicopters like the Chinook hasn't transformed the fundamentals of land warfare, but has certainly stepped up the pace. The ability to move forces and material rapidly like this is a tremendous resource for a task force commander.

the Siamese twins climbed tentatively into the air. Within seconds, the drogue—which was tied directly to the helicopter instead of to a swivel—twisted up and fouled. Then the load began to pitch up and down, slowly at first but with increasing vigor, until the lower helicopter threatened to hit the one above. At a thousand feet above Lawson Field, the crew chief pulled the red EMERGENCY JETTISON handle above the cargo hook, and several million dollars of sling load dropped straight down, landing neatly on its wheels. It was a hard landing, though, reducing the profile of the aircraft from its normal fourteen feet to about three.

The same technologies that have made the attack and observation helicopters so much more capable are used in the Chinook as well: an excellent navigation system will guide us to a spot where we can put some serious metal on the big bad wolf. From the point of view of the task force

A scout platoon climbs aboard a Chinook, the helicopter that first helped make airmobility a success way back in 1964, and is still going strong today.

93

commander and planning staff, the artillery raid is a great way to make a big dent in the opposition with little risk and low cost. A 155mm projectile makes an incredible mess when it lands: a not-very near miss can flip a main battle tank right over on its turret, and there are specialized warheads to wreak all sorts of havoc with the opposition. Of course the gun is so big that enemy commanders tend not to expect it to drop into their backyard, but that's what we're going to do right now.

As we approach the site for the "hip shoot," a small clearing in a dense forest, the job of the flight engineer becomes essential, because he will, in effect, land the load by telling us what to do. The bottom of the load is thirty feet below us, and we can't see it, so it is very difficult to know where it is without expert guidance. We gradually bleed off the airspeed until we are at a hundred-foot hover over the pasture where the gunners will set up shop, and the engineer begins his series of admonitions:

"Okay, sir, fifty feet—come forward ten and down slowly. Good, down ten, on the spot; down slow. Okay, twenty feet, looking good; ten feet, five feet—four, three, two, one, load's on the ground!" The pilot uses his pinky finger to depress one of the red buttons that embellish the cyclic control grip in his right hand, and the hook pops open and the "doughnut" falls out and onto the top of the ammunition trailer. Now the flight engineer brings us up again and over to where the gun will go, and we put that on the ground, careful to keep it from tilting forward with its tube in the dirt. It will be firing in a few minutes and the crew should not have to stop to clean it.

When the loads are both released, we slide off to the side and put the wheels lightly on the ground, and the crew dashes out the back.

"CLEAR!" reports the flight engineer, and it's back up on the collective and we're gone. We will park out of the way in a nearby clearing until we're summoned back. While we're waiting is a convenient time to refuel, and here comes the "mother cow" with her 300 gallons of JP-4 milk.

The boom of the big gun thunders through the forest, and then it's time to go back and get the kids. Playtime's over, time to hook up again! This time, though, we don't have anyone to help us on the ground, so the flight engineer will do the hookup by himself. First he positions us over the loads, then he uses a pole with a hook on one end to catch the doughnut, pulling it up and onto the cargo hook. Gosh, that was easy; now let's get the hell out of Dodge!

Back in the air we get a message on the secure radio that our scout platoon is ready to be picked up, and their location is specified with an eight-digit grid coordinate. Punch it into the GPS and we know exactly where they are, how to get there, and how long it will take to arrive. But all we say on the radio is "Roger." Even though the transmission is digitally encoded and is supposed to be secure, every time you key the transmitter you produce an emission that tells the whole wide world exactly where you are, if they are listening. We try not to take any more chances than the mission requires.

The gun and crew are delivered to their next place of business, and we are off to collect our scouts now that their good deeds are done.

We float above the treetops; it still feels like magic after all the years of doing it, the old pilots say. We move using nap-of-the-earth technique, as close to the ground as we can go, speeding up, slowing down, sometimes stopping for a look around to see if the coast is clear. It is, and we flare before landing on a low bluff just above the

sea. From out of nowhere appear the members of the scout platoon, who rush aboard like the practiced veterans they are, lugging weapons, packs, and radios. They're a hard-core bunch, and they need to be; they're going to a dangerous place, and we are going to deliver them.

Their platoon leader wedges his upper body into the cockpit and by yelling, pointing at the map, and gesturing emphatically we manage to confirm the LZ location despite the tremendous noise. The young lieutenant then goes back to see if he can find a seat in the no-smoking section. "CLEAR AFT!" You can hope and pray that none of those hand grenades or weapons goes off by accident back there. Up on the collective, for-

The high, hot flying conditions of the Mojave Desert make operations more difficult for some helicopters, but the Chinook's tremendous reserve of power lets it continue to provide delivery service for the troops.

ward cyclic, and off we go again, your basic battlefield taxi with another fare, headed for the bad part of town.

Our route will take us far from the airhead, into territory owned and operated by the enemy, but we won't go there directly. The CH-47 is very vulnerable to ground fire, and although our Delta has armor and a lot of redundancy for the various systems, we still need to fight smart. So we'll use cover, concealment, and a few sneaky tricks to take the boys out to play. We will follow ravines

A platoon of Australian infantry departs a CH-47 from the Iowa National Guard during a joint exercise involving American, Canadian, Australian, and British units. The helicopters have been busy most of the night delivering battalions of troops into little LZs like this one.

and valleys through the jungle, stay hidden within the terrain rather than trying to blunder boldly above it.

Miles from our LZ, we slip down into a clearing and land for a moment; the troops stay in their seats, though, and only someone closely observing will know that our insertion here is a deception. After thirty seconds on the ground, we're off again, then we repeat the maneuver out of sight of the first LZ. It is a great way to disguise the spot where our scouts will actually get off the bus and go to work.

After half a dozen fake insertions, we clear the trees ringing a steep and rocky hillside clearing, flare to kill forward airspeed, and come to a hover out of sight of anyone more than 200 meters away. Reason would tell you that no helicopter could land here, but we're not a conventional aircraft. Using our faithful and trusty friend in the back to guide us, we hover backward until our aft wheels are planted on an outcrop of boulders, and the scouts scurry out the ramp and off on their errands. They will occupy positions overlooking much of the island and will be able to observe and report to the task force commander what is happening in tremendous detail . . . if they survive. But this is their business, and ours is to drive this truck back to the barn for some gas, pick up the scouts again, and then move on to a new mission.

Our battalion has thoughtfully established a service station for us, not far from where we've been at work. It's a standard "forward area rearm and refuel point," which everybody just calls a FARRP. There are bladders of fuel and the pumps and hoses required to transfer it to our tanks. The flight engineer does the honors while we check on our next mission, which turns out to be a resupply effort for the infantry and will keep the aircraft busy far into the night.

Night operations have been possible for a long time, but several new technologies have made them really practical. With the old paper map approach to navigation, particularly at night or down low, it was hard to know where you were going or when you got there. But Doppler, Omega, and Global Positioning System navigation equipment has been added to the CH-47, allowing very accurate navigation under any conditions.

The Chinook in its current configuration is so easy to fly that a lot of new students with experience in other helicopters have difficulty adapting. The instructors have trouble making them let go of the controls, to allow the systems to do what they were designed to do—fly the airplane. Says one of the IPs,

It's easy to fly, if you'll let it do the work! Most of our students are coming to us from Hueys and 58s, and they are both very "hands on" kinds of airplanes. The controls are designed so that if they are displaced even a tenth of an inch, the computer receives a signal that the pilot wants to fly the airplane and stops all the nice features. But if you just set it up to do what you want and let go, it will maintain heading and attitude indefinitely. There's a trim button on top of the cyclic that you can use to change the attitude of the aircraft by just applying a little trim forward or aft. You can even roll it into a bank by applying lateral trim, and it will maintain that bank angle until it runs out of gas or you tell it to do something else.

The D model uses the shell and the concept behind the older Chinook, but applies a lot of lessons learned in Viet Nam, Grenada, and in the general evolution of American military aircraft. The maze of hydraulic lines, for example, has been reduced to mere hundreds of meters, and instead of running along the spine near the drive shaft, where they could leak on everything, two redundant sets are now routed along the sides of the cabin. Damage to one set doesn't put you out of business.

Aircraft availability has gone way up in a design that once had a reputation for maintenance problems, going from about 45 percent to better than 90 percent as the Deltas replaced the Bravos and Charlies. Unlike other Army helicopters, the CH-47 has a hands-off flight capability that provides some of the functions of an autopilot. Once you set up a heading and altitude, it will maintain them indefinitely. A seven-hour ferry flight will involve about fourteen minutes of hands-on flight for takeoffs and landings. Its load-carrying ability has evolved, too, from rated gross weight of 33,000 pounds for the A model to a 50,000-pound rating for the D, and one has lifted 54,000 pounds as a special event.

Although the Chinook is a cargo helicopter and is devoid of any offensive weapons systems, its IPs maintain that the aircraft has among the most complicated systems in the inventory to master, requiring seven weeks of instruction after a student has developed proficiency in another helicopter. Then the student learns to do it all over again, in the dark, with the lights off.

The flight engineer has his own instrument panel back by the ramp, with gauges to monitor the hydraulic systems and chip detector lights to warn of transmissions that are trying to disassemble themselves. His instruments are not duplicated in the cockpit, so his function becomes especially important.

One of the instructor pilots at Rucker sums up the virtues of the Chinook:

I've been flying these things for twenty years, and during all that time the main mission for this helicopter has been artillery support. As we get farther from the Viet Nam years and the experience we gained there, we forget what this helicopter is really good for, and that's logistics. It's hard to practice resupply in peacetime, but that's what our mission will probably be when we have another war. The tactical maneuver units of the Army are training for doing combat air assaults in the Black Hawks—but we're right in there behind them hauling in the new M198 howitzers and providing them with resupply. Basically, the mission hasn't really changed in all the years the CH-47 has been flying; the equipment we haul is bigger and heavier, but it's still the same kind of stuff. But one aspect is different; in Viet Nam you took off at the crack of dawn and flew all day and came home when it was dark. But now we're training for 24-hour operation, and if anything we're training for night operations more than for day, and that low-level flight that will help us survive in the mid-intensity kind of combat we expect. That's a real change from what was done before, and if somebody had told me, back in 1973, that we'd be flying down here in the trees—and doing all these missions in the dark of night, I think I'd have packed my bags and gone to dental school.

But I don't think our mission has really changed; we're still basically cargo. And I think it's the best mission in the Army. Those guys in the attack helicopters may get a hundred hours a year, and most of it is sitting out some place at a hover, looking for an enemy to engage. But for us, a mission involves a lot of adversity. We don't operate in a formation, so every pilot has to be able to navigate and talk on the radios, and it isn't a follow-the-leader or hover in the trees kind of job, so we're probably the most diverse pilots in the Army.

Air Assault—Black Hawk

It's difficult to find the location of Bravo Company, 3d Battalion, 123d Aviation Regiment, even in the bright light of midafternoon. But with a map and a set of good coordinates, you can get to the general area, and if you look around, you'll see the helicopters and the tents, stashed here and there between the trees and hills. The entire company area seems to be abandoned; except for a few soldiers working on aircraft, no one stirs. At last you find the camouflage nets and tents of the TOC where the S-3 sergeant says, "Sorry, sir, the commander is asleep right now. Everybody is. They flew all night."

The work of the UH-60 Black Hawks—the combat support role—is diverse and dangerous. They do all sorts of missions, except attack. They're big—easy to hit—and carry little armor. So they have to protect themselves, and the infantry they so often carry, using cover and concealment rather than brute force. That means low-level NOE flight, at maximum speed, at night. Nighttime is cheap armor; Americans have developed excellent night vision devices and dispense them to all and sundry. The people we fight don't have many of them, so they have a very hard time engaging high-speed, low-level targets. That doesn't mean they can't score points; it means that in darkness they score few, and have to work hard for those. So during the day the Black Hawk units rest (or try to), plot and scheme, eat, do paperwork, and maintain the helicopters. When darkness descends, they come to life and go to work.

While the pilots snooze and the crew chiefs

Short final for the landing zone—a flight of UH-60 Black Hawks flare for landing. The Black Hawk has replaced the venerable Huey as the basic battlefield bus for air assaults. With more speed, capacity, and armor, the Hawk is the foundation for many of the battle plans of the Army.

and mechanics pull maintenance, one officer is many kilometers away, receiving an order from the maneuver commander and his staff. The Black Hawks are needed tonight. They will provide a battlefield taxi service for a battalion of infantry. The mission is called an air assault and will deliver soldiers ready to fight, right on top of an objective.

The briefing starts at midnight. The air mission commander (AMC) tonight is a warrant officer with several thousand hours in the Black Hawk, much of it at night.

Twelve hours earlier, a battalion of infantry was inserted deep into enemy territory and an airhead was established. Since then, the infantry has secured the airhead and is ready to expand it. Artillery has been brought in by Chinooks and other Black Hawk units. The artillery has been reaching out and chewing on the enemy for hours, part of the plan to seize ground in the most efficient and economical way. But there is no substitute for infantry, and the maneuver commander has decided that it's time to take a bigger bite of the battlefield.

There are always going to be places that the enemy can't afford to defend, places where you can hit him without being hit too hard yourself. A commander can never be entirely sure where the enemy is, but he's paid to make winning bets. Tonight he wants his infantry moved out and into eight different grid squares, between five and ten kilometers from the airhead. The units will be small and vulnerable, but the massed artillery will be on call if they get into trouble.

We're tasked with the job of being the battlefield taxi service. The map and its overlays show the PZs (pick up zones) where we'll collect our passengers and the LZs (landing zones) where

Hmmm, I wonder what this thing is for? A crew chief checks the linkage on the UH-60's big rotor head. *George Hall photo.*

we'll deliver them. All the pilots carefully copy the information onto their own maps before the briefing begins and make copious notes while the AMC talks.

We'll crank up at 0200, take off at 0225, arrive at the first PZ at 0235. We'll be a flight of eight UH-60s, the last of which will be a spare in case we lose one – for any reason. The entire operation will be done in darkness, using night vision devices. There will be a thin overcast tonight, and a nearly full moon above that; illumination will be 87 percent.

The Black Hawk's panel is little different from the old Huey's, but the addition of the LED "chiclet" instruments for the engines have made life easier for pilots. The panel is bigger, though, and visibility somewhat less.

It's a couple of hundred meters from the TOC to the helicopter we will fly, and even though it's a fairly bright night, we've got to navigate carefully across the ground. Our flight tonight will involve the same careful navigation, except that we'll stay just above the trees and will fly from 40 to 140 knots. The helicopter was preflighted in

Get me outta here!!! Four Rangers are extracted from a hostile compound at Fort Bragg, North Carolina. The STABO technique isn't for the faint of heart or for normal circumstances, but it is a great way to leave the party when you've made a mess of things.

daylight and is good to go; the two M60 machine guns are mounted and the crew is already waiting for us. Time to get in and get settled.

The Black Hawk has a spacious cockpit, with a huge panel. The seats are large, comfy, covered in sheepskin, and surrounded by armor. The harness locks you firmly to the seat and makes you one with the airframe. Pull the straps tight, adjust the seat height so you can see where we're going, and make sure your feet can reach the pedals. We're just about set. Now for the helmet: the

One of the 7th Infantry Division's Hawk drivers studies the map and considers the novelty of flying in daylight. His unit spends much of its time in the field and deployed to places like Honduras and Panama. He usually sleeps during the day and works the graveyard shift.

AN/PVS-6 night vision goggles clip to a bracket on the front, the battery pack goes on the back, and a little cable connects the two. Be careful to assemble the components correctly, because if something comes loose later we could all have a problem!

The goggles are not very big and certainly not complicated to use, but they have revolutionized Army doctrine, on the ground and in the air. American soldiers (unlike those from some other cultures) have traditionally been reluctant to fly at night, but now that has changed. Darkness can provide protection for those who can learn to live with its hazards. The Army teaches all soldiers to work and fly at night, with and without the help of technology. You can fly a helicopter at night without goggles or other aids, and you can even do it down in the treetops if you are both brave and foolish, or desperate. Helicopter drivers expect to fly at night and at minimum altitudes just to survive in the next war. The basic problem is that low-level flight is dangerous enough in the daytime: there are wires everywhere, for instance, and wire strikes kill lots of helicopters. So let's not hit any wires tonight, okay?

Two 105mm howitzers are a light load for the UH-60 helping the "gun bunnies" with an artillery raid. The technique involves dropping into a handy spot with guns, ammo, and crews; shooting a few well-aimed rounds at the bad guys; then packing up before the rounds even hit the target.

Wait for me! A gun bunny dashes back to the bus after an artillery raid. With the gun crew back aboard, the helicopter will hover over the gun and the crew chief will reattach the sling. Then it's off for more adventure.

Day or night, the crews maintain the aircraft as well as fly in them, and hours in the field can be exceedingly long. Since nobody wants it to fall off, the rotor head comes in for special attention.

The goggles rotate down in front of your eyes and turn on automatically, revealing a bright, vivid green world in tremendous detail. Rotate them up again and you can see that it's *dark* out there! We'll go through the checklist and start procedures without them (they're for seeing outside the aircraft, not in), using the normal cockpit illumination. After the preliminaries, we fire up the APU, and the generators come on line and the hydraulic pressure climbs and stabilizes in the green. Now, the ENG 1 power lever comes out of OFF to IDLE and the START button is held in, and from behind you comes the rising pitch of the turbine as it starts to sing its song. The higher pitch of the little APU is displaced by the deeper voice of the number one engine. All its little

chiclets are glowing green and its life signs are all healthy, so now for ENG 2. It comes to life on request, happy and healthy, and we're almost in business. At the appointed minute the rotors are engaged and slowly start to revolve, quickly accelerating. The Hawk is fully alive, shimmering with nervous energy and power.

Down come the goggles: a look outside reveals seven other helicopters, all dressed up with someplace to go. The rotors of each twinkle brightly, the tips forming a sparkling disk visible only through the goggles. And it's a good thing we can see them, because we'll fly a tight formation through the gloom. Only half a rotor disk's distance may separate our blades from those of our friends over there, and one of the things you really want to avoid is getting ours mixed up with theirs. It makes a terrible mess.

If you keep your head up, you can look around and under the goggles to see the instruments and then back outside just by moving your eyes. It takes a little getting used to, but it works just fine. You've got to keep your head moving, however, because the field of view for the goggles is narrow. Keep up a good scan.

Okay, it's time to pull pitch: watch as the lead comes up and is followed by each helicopter in sequence. Wait until the aircraft in front of us clears the ground, then it's up on the collective and off we go! Over the radio comes a single word from the last aircraft in the flight. "FOXTROT" is all he says, the code word to let the flight leader know that all his ducks are in the air behind him, lined up nice and neat. We're off.

Ahead, the other Black Hawks float above the trees as the flight accelerates through seventy knots, looking like some exotic snake slithering above the terrain. We're about twenty feet above

"Stay over on your own side! These are *my* switches!!" Actually, checklist time is a cooperative affair: both pilots carefully assist each other with the ritual of aircraft preparation for flight.

the trees, and the flight blasts along, following the contours of the terrain rather than taking a direct course from A to B. We drop into a little valley that will shield us from unfriendly eyes and weapons — if the latest intel data is still current — and roar through the night toward the first PZ.

Off to the right and left appear Cobra gunships, our fighter escort. If anything nasty starts to happen, they'll be available to provide suppression. Even though they were intended to be daylight systems, they can be very effective at night

with their 70mm rockets and 20mm machine gun . . . and goggle-eyed gunners. They're supposed to be carrying a lot of nail rounds tonight, just one of which can take out a platoon of enemy infantry. It's nice to have them along.

Ten minutes out, flight lead turns into another

little valley. We all slow down in preparation for landing while the Cobras orbit protectively overhead. The PZ looks like a vacant pasture, a small one at that. We flare, come to a hover, and lower the collective to plant our wheels in the grass. Anybody home?

From the treeline dash squads of infantry, struggling with rucksacks and weapons. They've been briefed on which helicopter to board, and in less than sixty seconds all the helicopters are loaded. Flight lead is first off, and the rest of us

Business class, Black Hawk–style. These student Rangers are off for a few days in the woods, and for once they don't have to walk. The UH-60 can carry just about anything you can stuff inside, even a bunch of Rangers – if they're on their good behavior.

pull pitch in sequence. "FOXTROT!" is the call on the radio; on the road again!

The troops are jammed in back, freezing; the doors are open and it's breezy back there. That not only keeps the little puppies awake, it lets them get in and out as fast as possible. They hold their rucksacks on their laps and their weapons in one hand. On this airline, everybody carries guns and grenades. It is crowded with ten of them aboard; if we took the seats out and put straps across the doors, we could jam twenty-four in there (without rucks) and still fly the mission.

The formation closes up on the leader and we make a charge for the first LZ, another pasture about ten klicks into bad-guy country. A column of green dots floats into the sky over to the right—some enemy soldier firing randomly into the gloom at our sound. The tracers would be pretty if it were the Fourth of July, but it isn't—so they aren't. Somebody out there doesn't like us!

We follow rising ground toward a ridge line, blast across the top, and drop back down quickly. Some of the troops whoop and holler as the crest rushes past at 100 knots ten feet below in the scant moonlight; the experience is like a ride at Disneyland, but with real thrills and chills.

At 100 knots indicated airspeed, this Black Hawk skims the trees before sneaking into a little clearing on Fort Bragg's back lot. Then a squad of scouts will bail out for a few hours of fun and games with the opposition during the 82d Airborne Division's annual Market Square exercise.

Just minutes from lift-off, the formation starts to slow. Back on the cyclic, lower the collective, stay in sync with the helicopter fifty feet to our left front, and start looking for our spot. "ONE MINUTE!" yells the crew chief to the soldiers, and they tense for the command to exit. Some start to yell like maniacs, but what do you expect from infantrymen?

The LZ is supposed to be cold, and it is. No ground fire greets us. The infantry "un-ass" the bird, throw down rucks, and hit the ground two steps from the helicopter, rifles up and ready to defend us, just in case. Up on the collective and we're airborne again, off through the night, speed and darkness our faithful armor. Flight lead takes us back to the same PZ but by a slightly different route, just in case somebody wants to ambush us. Can't hurt to be sneaky, too.

Even with the goggles, this kind of operation is stressful, and after a few of these lifts you can start to feel a kind of fatigue seep into you. This is dangerous stuff. The formation is tight, and we are always a few seconds from collision with our brethren; add to that the possibilities of ground fire and the difficulty of navigation down low and it is understandable if you start to feel a little tense.

On the fourth lift, the lead makes a wrong turn. We fumble around for a few minutes trying to get oriented, then at last he sees the error of his ways and we line up for another delivery to another LZ. This time more green tracers illuminate the night, but our faithful friends, the

Fire mission: while the 105mm artillery rounds are still flying through space, a crew chief hooks the gun back onto the helicopter. The crew waits impatiently, their work done for the moment, before dashing off to another piece of vacant real estate to do it all again.

AH-1 Cobra drivers, are waiting for just such an invitation. We break off from the approach and orbit while the Cobras make a pass at the tree line with their 20mm machine guns, coming back for another run with rockets. We line up again for landing. The crew chief and gunner fire their M60s into the tree line, trying to suppress any unfriendly residents, and the red tracers hose the vegetation on both sides of the LZ. They wear night vision goggles (NVG) as well and can seek out bunkers and hiding places as well as in daytime.

This time the troops eject themselves from the helicopter as though they were spring-loaded. They hit the ground and start firing into the trees, but nothing comes back out. We're up and away in record time.

The AMC wants us to orbit for a few minutes to make sure the troops don't need to be extracted. Finally the infantry commander reports light resistance — nothing they can't manage. We can go home.

But first, let's find the FARRP and feed the bird a couple thousand pounds of JP-4 fuel and more ammo for the machine guns. Back in the safe, secure airhead we find the pasture that serves as a filling station, get in line, and wait our turn. Rotors still turning, the hose is connected and we take on a full load of fuel. Then, when everybody is topped off, we take off again for our home away from home. The sun will clear the horizon in twenty minutes, and the goggles are taken off and folded up.

Here's our parking spot. Down on the collective, tail wheel down, main gear down, and we're home again. We work through the shutdown checklist, item by item. Finally, power levels back to IDLE, check the clock, and wait two minutes while the engines cool. Then, levers back to OFF and quiet begins to descend on our consciousness. Gradually apply the rotor brake until the blades stop turning, and the silence is deafening. It's time for chow. Then I'm going to sleep all day!

UH-60 BLACK HAWK

The Black Hawk was the first of the new generation of helicopters to come out of Viet Nam, carrying more of everything, faster and farther, with more reliability and more precise navigation than anything that came before it. The UH-60 Black Hawk is a Sikorsky product, a utility helicopter with two engines, four blades, a range of about 600 kilometers (360 miles), and a cruise speed of about 140 knots. It normally carries a crew of three or four — two pilots and one or two crew. If helicopters like the Apache and the OH-58 D are interesting because their systems are so complicated and capable, then the Black Hawk is interesting because its *missions* are so complicated and capable of influencing the battle.

The Black Hawk is really just a new and much-improved Huey, that faithful and versatile friend of the soldier that could do just about everything just about everywhere. The United States fought a war with the Huey, and there are still lots around. Almost all the remaining combat vets have hours in them, and the design is a bench-

The real world is full of hazards that you might encounter once in a career — on your last mission. The simulator is a place to experience the worst disasters in aviation and still walk away, perhaps with some life-saving skills and knowledge. *George Hall photo.*

mark for newer helicopters. Although the Huey will probably stay in the inventory for a long time, its missions mostly have been assumed by the Black Hawk. A veteran Huey driver compares the two.

The Black Hawk is a "lead sled"! Unless you try to fill it with gold bars, there is nothing else that will gross it out. You can pull the seats out and stack people in there until it's full—and still fly! There is a rush to all that power; it's always there when you need it. When you move the controls, the airplane moves—now! The hook is good for eight thousand pounds, and as long as you're close, you can lift it, even the new HUMVEE [a utility vehicle], which is right up there. For a helicopter pilot to go from a 90-knot Huey to be able to go someplace at 160 knots is just incredible. When they came out with the specs for the Black Hawk it showed only 1.8 hours of fuel for mission time, and I thought that was ridiculous. I was still thinking in terms of 90 knots. When you crank it up to 140 knots, you get a lot more done. So it's got plenty of gas.

The power and responsiveness are the major improvements, and they go together. It gets you out of trouble a lot quicker. If you screw up an approach to an LZ, you've got a lot of troops aboard and you're a little bit too fast, you still have lots of power to stop yourself.

The other thing is the twin engine syndrome; anytime something goes wrong there's not the panic that can happen when something goes wrong in a Huey. Then, you have to find a place to land, NOW. When you're over the ocean, it doesn't look too swell. But with the Black Hawk there's another engine there, no matter what the emergency. You've got more time to work with it and you tend to stay a lot calmer.

When I was in the 101st I was part of the "cav" and we had our own organic infantry element that we always used, as opposed to an assault company where you serve everybody. Air assault doctrine means putting the troops as close to the enemy as possible. We do a lot more at night with night vision goggles. We just got back from JRTC where we did lots of night raids of different kinds—in fact we tried to do all our operations at night. If you can't be seen, you can't be shot. The first thing we did at JRTC was to help the division establish itself in the area. My company flew a deception mission by doing a series of false insertions moving away from the actual area of advance. Another mission we did involved putting troops right on top of an enemy supply dump— again at night under the goggles. And then we helped assault a fortified position by lifting troops to within about a thousand meters of the objective and then putting a mortar team into a separate position nearby where they could provide fire support.

All night long we had four Black Hawks hauling barrier material, stakes, concertina wire, lumber, from the battalion support area (BSA) up to the front. The infantry companies set up their own little LZs and we ferried this material in to them. When the enemy tanks showed up the next morning their advance was slowed tremendously, and that let our guys pick them off in the engagement areas with a lot more precision than if they had been steaming through.

Perhaps the most important of these Black Hawk missions involves delivering people to important places at important times under difficult conditions. When these missions are done in large numbers, the Army calls it an air assault or an airmobile operation; the first involves putting soldiers right on top of the

enemy, whereas the second involves getting them close and letting them walk the last few hundred meters. Both of these missions fall under the general description of "combat support," because no matter how many bullet holes they put in your helicopter, you are not using your helicopter to directly engage the enemy, but to help someone else as they attack. While it might not seem as glamorous as busting tanks with Hellfire missiles, it can mean more to the maneuver commander's success or failure.

The Air Force and Navy get paved runways and radio navigation aids; the Army gets a nameless clearing in the trees, perhaps spiced by a welcoming committee with machine guns. Rangers are delivered to a remote exercise area at Fort Benning. They will walk the 20 miles back.

The concept of air assault operations is an evolution of the old airborne ideas. Basically, it is a way to fight the enemy anywhere on the battlefield, without worrying about terrain features that stop or slow other kinds of maneuvers. It mixes aviation and infantry in a powerful, flexible, and integrated way as part of a way of fighting that the

Army calls AirLand Battle. The ground commander uses aviation within his concept of a larger mission to provide firepower and mobility quickly and in mass, destroying enemy forces or seizing key terrain.

AIR ASSAULT

The units that perform this mission are usually organized as assault helicopter battalions (AHBs), and they are typically found supporting divisions

Hooking up after an artillery raid. It's a lot easier in daylight than at night when it is usually done. Then, everybody wears night vision goggles and everybody sweats.

or corps. They give senior commanders and their staff a highly mobile, flexible, and responsive combat force.

An AHB does lots of things for its bosses: move combat power around rapidly, including troops, supplies, and equipment; conduct air assaults and air movements; assist with command

120

and control; and perform medevacs and intel missions. It is most effective when it operates as part of the "combined arms team," delivering forces at critical times and places. The AHB lets a division or corps attack the enemy from all directions as AirLand Battle doctrine suggests: with initiative, depth, agility, and synchronization.

Although AHBs can do lots of missions, the air assault is their forte. They are masters of the art, a complicated and expensive art at that. Air assaults are big-risk, big-payoff missions; if they go well, they make a big difference. Small air assaults on Grenada were used to rescue the medical students from their campus. An air assault on the Son Tay prison camp deep inside North Viet Nam was another audacious use of the technique. Air assaults were an early and common use of helicopters in Viet Nam and had a profound influence on the battles, both for the VC and NVA as well as all the friendly forces.

The cyclic control tilts the rotor disk and requires most of the pilot's attention. The trigger operates the radio and ICS (intercom); the black button on top is for cyclic trim; the black hook near the pinky finger releases the cargo hook.

Military organizations are not democracies; they're dictatorships. The dictator in a fight is the senior guy on the local ground, the one man who's responsible to the commander in chief if things go right or wrong. When an air assault is being considered, it is considered only as one part of a ground tactical plan. Depending on the mission, either the ground or air commander will be in charge of the operation. The air assault task force commander (AATFC) controls a force that is put together to achieve a specific mission, combining all the appropriate elements of the combined arms team: infantry, artillery, air defense, aviation, and engineers. The process of mixing and matching these resources is called "task organization," and yields in this case a task force. The mission is usually the delivery of troops—a company, a battalion, a brigade—to a location, generally close to the enemy.

The AATFC specifies when he wants it to happen, and with that information the S-3 shop starts what they call a "reverse planning sequence." If he wants to send a company out and have them on the LZ at 0500 tomorrow, great, no problem! If he wants them to be there in two hours, it will be a goatscrew. The S-3 staff starts by looking at what the AATFC wants to do on the ground—the ground tactical plan; that will dictate where and when the helicopters will land, which in turn dictates how and when they will have to move from the PZ to the LZ, which in turn requires a plan for loading the aircraft and for staging the troops and helicopters prior to the assault. It gets very complicated, with lots of ducks to line up, and the more complicated the mission the more time the S-3 guys want to prepare. They never get enough. And what looks good on the map isn't necessarily what looks good on the ground, so it's a good idea to have alternate plans.

An S-3 says: "The pilot wants to know when we're picking up the troops and where we're dropping them off; if he gets shot down, where does he go, who's going to pick him up, where are the bad guys and what their capabilities are, where fuel and food are. So the more time you have to plan the mission, the better the mission comes off."

Air assault operations can use any infantry forces, but Rangers, light infantry, airborne, and air assault infantry are preferred, since these units have been trained specifically for this kind of mission. To do a full-scale air assault usually requires the planning assets of a division, and that's why the 101st Airborne Division (Air Assault) is considered the master of the art. But when air assault operations go badly, you can lose a lot of your assets just as fast, and that means lots of dead and wounded people and aircraft. But used wisely, such an operation can win a war.

If you happen to be a TF commander, you're always struggling with limits: limited numbers of people, of weapons, of supporting artillery, and always of those minutes that keep ticking away. But with enough Black Hawks and people who know what to do with them, you can mass your "combat power" from one place to another, quickly. That helps accomplish something that has been valuable since cavemen used the good old club, hand, M1, to beat on each other—the element of surprise. Helicopters give you flexibility, mobility, and speed—and that lets you gain and maintain the initiative. The other side will have to dance to your tune. You can then attack and make him defend. And helicopters let you attack across a wide, deep, broad battlefield. Since you can strike almost anywhere, he has to defend everywhere, and that spreads him thin. But, more than any other Army aviation mission, the air assault requires far more detailed planning to keep friendly blood from mixing with enemy.

There are two guys who are crucial to any air assault: the air assault task force commander and the air mission commander. The AATFC is the big boss for the Army show, probably a colonel or brigadier general. The air mission commander can be any pilot in the unit, and in training everybody does the job from time to time. In combat, though, it will be someone who knows his business very, very well.

Another critical job is that of the flight leader. When the assault aircraft take off, each formation plays follow the leader, and the guy up front not only has to find his way to the objective, he needs to adjust his speed so that the parade arrives on time for the big show. So flight lead is always the best navigator in the unit, regardless of rank. The AMC will be somewhere behind him, often in the number three position.

And if the TF is lucky enough to get some protection, an attack helicopter unit will be assigned to the mission, its Cobras or Apaches out in front and on the flanks, beating up the enemy air defenses, putting suppressive fire on the LZ, overwatching the LZ in case the bad guys try to reinforce, and functioning as a reserve if motorized or armored forces are part of the threat.

Then there's the problem of resupply. A unit engaged in combat consumes tremendous quantities of food, ammunition, fuel, and other supplies; ground units get these commodities through their "combat trains." Air assault units need resupply too, but it is harder to do when the enemy is in the way or there are no roads available. So resupply is done by using the LOGPAC method; all the

Up to a hover, then the cyclic goes forward, pull in some pitch, and we're outta here! A hard-working UH-60 from the 17th Aviation Brigade provides round-the-clock delivery service for its parent, the 82d Airborne.

ammunition and food needed for individual companies are prepackaged and ready for delivery by air. The loads are small enough for Black Hawks to carry externally, even though the cargo hook on the UH-64 is rated only to 8,000 pounds.

The Black Hawk has proved itself a rightful descendant of the famous and fabled Huey. It's a strong and dependable battlefield bus that gives maneuver commanders mobility and flexibility when they fight the AirLand Battle. While there's little chance anybody will try to make a gunship out of this aircraft, it does just about everything else with style and grace, moving troops, supplies, and equipment quickly and safely across the battlefield. It even gets tricked out in special editions for electronic warfare, psychological warfare, and medical evacuation missions. As one Black Hawk driver says, "This is the best helicopter the Army ever bought!"

Army Air in the Future

Since the first Army aviators took to the sky during the early battles of the Civil War, a lot has changed, and a lot has stayed pretty much the same. The fundamental nature of warfare is loaded with constants, although every new conflict will probably be different than the participants expected. Right now, the Army has invested tremendous amounts of money and imagination in systems and in SOPs for fighting the next war, and the scenario that opens this book is one kind of fight that may someday actually happen. There are lots of people, however, who firmly believe that such missions are unrealistic and could never succeed in the high-threat environment of a modern, large-scale battlefield. Others think that such a battlefield will never be seen because the world has shrunk so much that big wars between big powers are unlikely. Still others contend that the complexity of systems like those of the AH-64 makes them unreliable and unsuited for combat in little jungle conflicts far from the maintenance depots. Well, they may be right; the Air Force discovered in the middle 1960s that its aircraft were quite unsuited to the needs of Viet Nam, and they improvised like crazy until new designs could be fielded. Maybe that will happen again. There's only one way to find out, and that is to wait and see.

The Army currently is giving a great deal of attention to small encounters with local bullies with an expanding role for the special operations community; within that branch is a whole gaggle of specially equipped and trained aviators (many of whom are associated with Task Force 160 out of Fort Campbell, Kentucky), working mostly in secret. Their equipment and planning have been tested recently in the Persian Gulf, where Army helicopters were the weapon of choice against Iranian gunboats, with excellent results. So, although Army aviation has been considered something of a second-class citizen in the military community during the post–Viet Nam era, this is, to my mind, an unfair and inappropriate assessment. The missions of Army aviation are tremendously significant to the nation, and very demanding of the organizations that have to perform them. I am convinced they can perform their designated wartime missions, perhaps better than the critics will fare with their own missions.

Soldiers have expressions for talking about The Next Time. "When the balloon goes up . . ." is one. Any casual look at the past suggests that every couple of decades the balloon does indeed go up, and the services of the armed forces are required. There will be another war, sooner or later, bigger or smaller, against a group of nations or against a few terrorists. Army aviation will probably play a role in the fight.

Current American military doctrine still depends fundamentally on the ultimate weapon—the individual infantry rifleman—to win the war. And the individual rifleman, to do his job, will have to have a lot of support. That support will come first and foremost from Apaches, Cobras, Black Hawks, Chinooks and Kiowas. Army aviation will provide the close air support the soldiers need—transport into battle, fire support, casualty evacuation, command and control, observation, resupply, and all the rest. In any kind of conflict, AirLand Battle will challenge all the players in

The AH-64 Apache represents a trend in military aircraft design: extremely complicated, sophisticated, expensive systems that can accomplish wonders—when they work and until they are shot down. Can we pay for enough to do the job? *George Hall photo.*

The old Cobra has been upgraded by the penny-pinching Marines into a modern attack helicopter at far less cost than that of the Apache. Some Army aviators think the AH-1 upgrade was a smarter move than buying costly AH-64s.

The Chinook in its upgraded Delta model remains a foundation for the Army's combat support and combat service support missions, 30 years after it appeared on Boeing's drafting tables.

ways no training ever can; it remains to be seen how effective the systems, doctrine, and training will be.

So, time will tell. But someday in the future, our soldiers will load up and deploy. At some ungodly hour on some black night, the APUs will all light off at the appointed second. Turbine engines will spin to life and fill the air with the perfume of jet exhaust; cold machines will come to life and rotors start to turn. Scared and nervous men will ride off into all sorts of missions. Hellfire missiles will slide off the rails, rockets will slither from the tubes, green tracers will come up and red tracers go down. Black Hawks will deliver battalions of soldiers to LZs deep in enemy territory. Chinooks will deliver guns and ammunition to mountaintops. Apaches and Cobras will seek out and engage the forces of evil. Kiowas will find the enemy miles away

through dark and fog. The men and the machines will all be tested in that ultimate training exercise, the real world. Some will pass, some will fail.

It has been a long time since anyone has shot at me, particularly while riding in a helicopter. But I still remember the soldiers, officers and enlisted, who flew with me back in the early days of the war in Viet Nam, who accomplished their missions in spite of inadequate aircraft, inappropriate rules of engagement, near misses, death and destruction. They did their work with quiet calm and amazing humor under the worst of circumstances. These men were an inspiration, one that has endured the decades. The Army seems to be able to find and develop the kind of people who rise to the challenge and thrive on adversity. These men and women have been the foundation of the Army and Army aviation since each began, and will be its foundation in the future.

Inventory of Weapons

A quartet of Hellfires hung on an Apache's stubby little pylon. Two of the missiles have active seekers, and two are for show, not go. The real thing is seldom fired, but the gunners believe their training is so realistic that these are sufficient—except when bad guys are really at the door.

HELLFIRE MISSILE

The origins of the AGM-114A Hellfire go back to 1964, when the limitations of the wire-guided missile were already obvious and development of a "fire-and-forget" missile was begun. It hasn't finished yet, but the Hellfire is as close as we're going to get for the near future.

The Hellfire is a laser-seeking missile that can recognize and home on a coded image of laser light, and the laser can come from anybody, not just the source of the missile. The United States and NATO allies have lots of laser designators all over the battlefield in order to make life happy for attack helicopter drivers, among others.

In 1988, when the cold war began to thaw a bit, a Soviet general visited Fort Hood and was treated to a demonstration of the Apache helicopter and the Hellfire missile. Before his arrival, one of the AH-64 companies was selected to put on the show and tasked to provide its best pilots and gunners. Well, the Hellfire costs too much, at $30,000, to fire very often, and nobody in the whole company had fired one outside of the simulator. So the gunners with the best simulator scores were selected. To the horror of the brass arranging the show, they turned out to be a couple of fresh-faced young warrant officers hardly out of flight school. There were loud protests from above, but the company commander stuck to his gunners, and on the appointed day the Soviet watched three Hellfires launched by the Apaches at three (American M48) tanks. All three scored solid hits, and the inner thoughts of the visitor were not recorded.

M65 TOW MISSILE

Ever since people have insisted on hiding inside those big heavy sardine cans called tanks, running around and making a mess of the neighborhood, other people have been trying to make them come out and behave. At first all it took was a bigger bullet, then a little artillery round, after which came high-velocity artillery. By the end of World War II, armor was getting to be six or eight inches thick and the only practical calling card was a shaped charge.

The TOW is a tube-launched missile, optically guided from start to finish by two wires that trail out the back. It is a design from the 1960s, fielded in 1970, and worked on the battlefield of the time, but is a little out of date now. The speed of the missile is rather slow, and it can take ten or more seconds to move from A to B, during which time the gunner wishes he were somewhere else. When it fires, a large, bright flash tells all and sundry where you are and what you're doing—neither of which improves your life expectancy. The range of the TOW is limited by the length of the wires, and they are not as long as people on the modern battlefield would like. Engagements are at longer and longer ranges, and the TOW is getting to be inadequate for a lot of antiarmor missions. It's still useful for bunker busting, but you'd better hope the other team doesn't have heat-seeking missiles or high-velocity ADA when you decide to drop in for a little attitude adjustment.

The basic missile has received several upgrades over the years, and now is considered effective to about 3,700 meters. And the TOW2 is supposed to defeat composite and reactive armor.

The TOW gets bolted to all sorts of vehicles and even shoots from a tripod on the ground. But the airborne version that is carried by helicopters is essentially the same weapon as the ground forces use.

The improved TOW costs less to manufacture than a Hellfire, so there will be more of them around for a while. Depending on the type of missile, the TOW can reach out to about four kilometers (two and a half miles), although it takes twenty-two seconds to get there—an eternity under the wrong conditions.

This Stinger provides a cheap, light, air-to-air capability for Army aviation—a new idea that has taken some getting used to. The missile is alleged to have been used successfully from OH-58 Kiowas in the Persian Gulf. *Doug Zalud Photo/Arms Communications.*

STINGER MISSILE

The air-to-air mission is one that hasn't been a worry to Army pilots over the years, according to doctrine, because our brothers in arms, the dear old USAF, would be overhead keeping the skies clean of airborne threats to friendly helicopters. That assumption is changing. The Soviets already have excellent combat helicopters, like the Hind, with capabilities similar to the Apache, and there are reports that they are developing a helicopter dedicated to killing NATO and U.S. helicopters. People are starting to give some serious thought to ways of dealing with such a threat, and the obvious off-the-shelf option is the Stinger missile, a combat-proven system for dealing with enemy air. In the ground version, it weighs only thirty-five pounds in a package that's only 2.75 inches in diameter and 5 feet long. Once the system is powered up and pointed at a heat source (like a jet engine), the seeker in the warhead locks onto the source; when it's fired, it just chases the heat source until it bumps into it, then the warhead explodes and the plane falls out of the sky.

The Stinger has been delivered to Afghan forces and they in turn have offered it to the Soviet Mi-23 Hinds overhead, with a kill rate exceeding 50 percent—excellent results. Until the Stinger arrived, the Soviet helicopters flew anywhere, anytime—and afterward they stayed in the pattern. The system has received a lot of credit for encouraging the Soviet withdrawal.

The Stinger is a light system and could be used on virtually any Army helicopter to deal with enemy helicopter or "fast mover" threats. It has been fired from OH-58s, a modification called ATAS (air-to-air Stinger). The rumor mill says this has already been done to the 58s operating in the Persian Gulf, and that they have been successfully used against Iranian aircraft.

2.75-inch (70mm) HYDRA 70 FOLDING FIN AERIAL ROCKET

Rockets are forever in warfare, and the 2.75-inch version goes back nearly that far. Its first use on helicopters began on H-13s and H-34s in the 1950s, when crews experimented with "field expedient" designs to beat up the enemy. The 2.75-inch rockets are what the military calls "area" weapons, meaning that they are intended to saturate a target area with multiple hits rather than sending one off to slide through a bunker aperture. The rocket is basically a very simple device—a tube packed with solid propellant that burns for a second or so when ignited by an electrical charge.

The current version looks a lot like its predecessor, which is too bad, because it is far more accurate and effective. The old rocket had a tendency to wander, and was an area weapon no matter what you needed. The new Hydra 70 system is a precision device that is cheap, reliable, fast, and accurate. It packs twice the energy into the same 70mm package, and turns it loose in half the time. It spins more than 2,000 rpm in flight, which provides tremendous stability, with a range out to more than 8 kilometers at a speed of 750 meters per second. If you want to cover a large area, you've got to program the system to shoot at a large area.

As good as the Mark 66 motor is, perhaps the big improvement has to do with the pointy end. There are half a dozen kinds of warheads available, including the multipurpose submunition round, a shaped-charge version for killing light armor, the flechette warhead for troops, a smokescreen round for providing a place to hide, and an illumination round for putting a little light on the subject on a cold, dark night. There's even a chaff round to spoof enemy radars. But the plain vanilla version for decades has been the high-explosive warhead.

M230 30mm CHAIN GUN

The chain gun is found beneath the nose of the Apache helicopter, put there by designers who wanted the pilots to have something to engage the numerous light armor vehicles the crew might

The 20mm machine gun can put a lot of steel on the target. It will reach out about one mile and is designed for "soft" targets like unarmored vehicles, lightly fortified positions, and people.

The business end of the M230 chain gun is a bad place to be when push comes to shove. That hole is over an inch wide, and big chunks of steel and explosive come pumping out at the rate of ten a second.

confront in a major European war. The Hellfire missiles are too precious for anything but the heavy armor of main battle tanks and occasional other point targets. But the crew needs something to discourage the opposition while they are busy disassembling their tanks. The chain gun is available for any such threats and its big bullets (more than an inch in diameter) can kill all kinds of antiaircraft systems, BMPs, BRDMs, and of course trucks and other thin-skinned targets, including people. The Apache carries 1,200 rounds, and they are squirted out at the rate of about 600 per minute. The pilot can operate the chain gun while the gunner is busy keeping his Hellfires burning.

20mm CANNON

Found on the Cobra, this is the baby brother to the 30mm chain gun. The maximum effective range is only 2,000 meters (about a mile). At that range the bullets still have enough energy to detonate the little wad of explosive inside, spreading shrapnel for several meters in every direction. They were designed for light armor and unarmored vehicles like trucks, back in an era when the heat-seeking missile was just a gleam in the eye of some Soviet designer.

7.62-inch MACHINE GUN

The Black Hawk mounts two of these for self-protection, primarily to keep the heads of the opposition down while getting in and out of an LZ. While an M60 may look big and bad when Rambo is slinging one around, it's the baby of the systems on helicopters. Its effective range is only 1,100 meters, its rate of fire is comparatively slow, and the tracers burn out after 900 meters; but you still don't want to get shot by one.

Glossary

ADA Air defense artillery, the gun and missile systems that take a lot of the joy out of life for helo drivers.

AH- Attack helicopter prefix.

AHB Assault helicopter battalion, typically three companies of UH-60s and a headquarters group—about 45 aircraft and 160 people.

Attrit To inflict damage, to make (or suffer) losses, attrition.

Baby grand Maneuver performed when a helicopter loses power and flight control and comes zooming out of the sky just like a baby grand piano.

Bad boy Any item of equipment that is admired for its technical sophistication or brute power; also applied to items whose name the speaker has momentarily forgotten.

Beach ball Mast-mounted sight (MMS) used on the OH-58 D helicopter.

Breaking 90 Rolling more than 90 degrees in a Black Hawk, an exhilarating and unauthorized maneuver.

Cav Cavalry; in aviation, a unit that performs traditional cavalry missions, such as screening, reconnaissance, et cetera.

CH- Cargo helicopter prefix.

Chiclets Little LED (light-emitting diode) lights now used to show engine condition, replacing the old gauges.

Clean your clock To kill or take apart.

Combined arms team Integrated effort of infantry, artillery, aviation, engineers, and armor.

CPG Co-pilot/gunner, the front seat occupant in Apache and Cobra attack helicopters. The CPG's primary job is to engage targets with the weapons of the aircraft. He can also fly the aircraft if necessary.

Dash 10 Operator's manual.

Doughnut Eye of the sling that engages the cargo hook under helicopters.

ECM Electronic countermeasures.

EW Electronic warfare, including jamming and deception.

FARRP Forward area rearm and refuel point.

Fast mover Tactical jet aircraft from the Air Force, Navy, or Marines.

FEBA Forward edge of battle area, the demarcation between friendly and enemy forces during active combat.

FLIR Forward-looking infrared, a sensor system that "sees" the world in patterns of hot and cold, rather than light and dark. Used in Apache and Kiowa helicopters.

FLOT Forward line of own troops; an important expression in wartime.

GPS Global positioning system, a highly accurate navigation technology.

Green-eyed and silly Effect of prolonged, continuous use of night vision goggles with their green image.

Guns Gunships; attack helicopters such as the Apache and Cobra.

HMD Helmet mounted display.

ICS Internal communication system, the intercom the crew uses to talk to each other.

IHADS Integrated helmet and display sight system. A very complex technology that lets a pilot or gunner look in any direction out of the cockpit and still see instrument displays. The system also permits the aiming of weapons systems (within limits) by just looking at a target.

IP Instructor pilot, the guy who gives you your check ride.

Klick Kilometer; a thousand meters, or about six-tenths of a mile, the standard unit of distance in the new metric Army.

Knot Measure of airspeed, slightly more than a mile, generally expressed as knots indicated airspeed (KIAS); 100 knots equals about 110 miles per hour.

LOGPAC Logistics package; a prepackaged set of supplies for a unit in combat, combining ammunition, food, and fuel ready for air movement as an external or internal load.

Mask/unmask To use terrain for concealment; to reveal weapons and sights, usually to fire.

MMS Mast-mounted sight, the "beach ball" sensor assembly that is mounted above the rotor head on the OH-58 D Kiowa.

Mother cow Helicopter whose mission is to carry fuel for others, usually in a 500-gallon bladder carried as an external load.

MPSM Multipurpose submunition, one of the many warheads available for the Hydra 70 rocket.

NBC Nuclear, biological, chemical warfare—the dirtiest part of the modern threat battlefield.

NOE Nap of the earth flight, usually ten to twenty feet above the trees.

OH- Observation helicopter prefix.

Passage point Location where your side will probably refrain from killing you when you return from a mission into enemy territory.

PIC Pilot in command.

Rocket ride/rock and roll/brush hogging Fast and hairy flying—great fun and rather dangerous.

Rotorhead/airdale Derisive names applied to aviators by ground-crawling slime.

Rotorwash Evil combination of spirituous liquors consumed only on ceremonial occasions.

SEAD Suppression of enemy air defenses.

Serial Group of helicopters that are part of an air assault operation; five helicopters may be one of four serials in a lift.

Six-million-dollar paperweight Black Hawk hangar queen.

Slick Troop-carrying version of the UH-1, so called because of its smooth sides. The gunship version had a variety of weapons bolted to the skids.

Slimes Faint little aircraft position lights used to maintain tactical formation at night, invisible except at close range.

Slug UH-1 Huey.

SOP Standard operating procedure, a kind of general purpose order that is published far in advance of need. SOPs tell a unit how to deal with most situations without having to go ask the boss.

Squadron Aviation and cavalry expression for what everybody else calls a battalion, i.e., three companies and a headquarters.

Tac E Tactical emergency.

TADS Target acquisition and designation system, the latest gee-whiz hardware, part of the AH-64 Apache.

TOC Tactical operations center; the little headquarters where missions are planned and briefings are usually given.

TOW Tube-launched, optically tracked, wire-guided missile, used from the ground and air against point targets such as tanks and bunkers.

Troop Traditional designation for a cavalry company–sized unit.

UH- Utility helicopter prefix.

About the Author/Photographer

Hans Halberstadt is a writer and photographer specializing in military subjects. He has an abiding interest in life-or-death issues that began during a tour in Viet Nam as a helicopter gunner. He lives in San Jose, California. Previous books include USCG: ALWAYS READY, AIRBORNE: ASSAULT FROM THE SKY, GREEN BERETS: UNCONVENTIONAL WARRIORS, and NTC: A PRIMER OF MODERN LAND COMBAT.